POETRY ROCKS!

Early British Poetry

"Words That Burn"

Paula Johanson

Enslow Publishers, Inc.
40 Industrial Road
Box 398
Berkeley Heights, NJ 07922
USA
http://www.enslow.com

For my dear bear heart

"Poetry is thoughts that breathe, and words that burn."
—Thomas Gray

Library of Congress Cataloging-in-Publication Data

Johanson, Paula.

Early British poetry, "words that burn" / Paula Johanson.
      p. cm. — (Poetry rocks!)
Includes bibliographical references and index.
Summary: "Examines early British poetry from the 7th century into the 19th century, including short biographies of poets like William Shakespeare and John Donne; also examples of poems, poetic techniques, and explication"—Provided by publisher.
ISBN-13: 978-0-7660-3276-7
ISBN-10: 0-7660-3276-0
1. English poetry—History and criticism—Juvenile literature. 2. Poets, English—Biography—Juvenile literature. I. Title.
PR502.J59 2010
821.009—dc22   2008053657

Printed in the United States of America

10 9 8 7 6 5 4 3 2 1

To Our Readers: We have done our best to make sure all Internet addresses in this book were active and appropriate when we went to press. However, the author and the publisher have no control over and assume no liability for the material available on those Internet sites or on other Web sites they may link to. Any comments or suggestions can be sent by e-mail to comments@enslow.com or to the address on the back cover.

♻ Enslow Publishers, Inc., is committed to printing our books on recycled paper. The paper in every book contains 10% to 30% post-consumer waste (PCW). The cover board on the outside of each book contains 100% PCW. Our goal is to do our part to help young people and the environment too!

Illustration Credits: Clipart.com, pp. 64, 72, 119, 124, 141; Corel Corp., pp. 5, 11, 21, 31, 42, 51, 62, 71, 80, 91, 101, 110, 120, 129, 140; Everett Collection, pp. 12, 36, 41, 89; Library of Congress, pp. 22, 52, 60, 92, 103; Photos.com, pp. 46, 83, 108, 123, 126, 130, 135, 145.

Cover Illustration: Corel Corp.

Grateful acknowledgment is made for permission to reprint the following copyrighted works: "The Ruin," "Wulf and Eadwacer," and "Riddle 30" from THE FIRST POEMS IN ENGLISH, translated and edited by Michael Alexander (Translations first published 1966, revised and expanded 1991. This edition first published in 2008). Copyright © Michael Alexander 1966, 1977, 1991, 2008. Reproduced by permission of Penguin Books Ltd.

Contents

INTRODUCTION

People use words in many ways, but poetry has always been something special. We can all count objects and make lists, we can ask someone to do something or write a letter, we can talk about plans or keep business records—but poetry is different from all those uses of language. Poetry, whether spoken aloud or written down, uses words in ways that are more significant than a casual conversation. Poets use words to impress the listeners with a shared experience that connects us to each other, to our shared past, and to the world around us. Because of this, poems are deeply meaningful in both a personal sense and a cultural sense. For some people, poetry is regarded as having magical or spiritual strength to inspire us to do well. But even people who say they do not like or understand poetry know the importance of singing a national anthem or making wedding vows, using formal words.

Poetry in English originated during the Middle Ages, when people first began speaking a language recognizable as English. It did not sound exactly like what we speak today, modern English. Old English, or Anglo-Saxon, was the tongue of the Angles and the Saxons. These were tribes of people who invaded the British Isles around the year 400 C.E. (Common Era). Old English was a dialect of what later became Low German. The language changed a little during the invasion, as some words were adapted from the Celtic dialects previously spoken in Britain. Poetry chanted aloud was an important part of the Anglo-Saxon culture, as they had very few written records.

Poetry written in English began when the Anglo-Saxons converted to Christianity. Christian monks wrote versions of some Old English poetry, but over the years, most of this poetry was lost. Only four books with a few of these poems were preserved. Oral poetry chanted aloud continued to be part of daily life for over a thousand years.

With the Norman Conquest in 1066, the language began changing. The Normans spoke French, and their language had a strong influence on how everyone in Britain spoke and wrote. While educated people were writing in Latin and keeping records in Latin or French, oral poetry in English continued to be popular. The Anglo-Saxon language became what we now call Middle English, which is a lot easier for modern readers to understand than Anglo-Saxon.

The population began shifting from rural farms into the small towns and cities. Literacy increased dramatically about 1200 C.E. By 1300 there was a great deal of literature being written in English. Most of these poems and songs and stories were meant for a popular audience and were written by people with only a modest education. The vowels began shifting slowly around this time so that *mouse* and *mice* were no longer pronounced "moose" and "meese." Gradually, some consonants also became silent.

The Renaissance came later to England than to Italy and France, around 1485. English intellectuals felt this delay keenly and worked to enrich and renew their own country's literature and culture. The language was changing again, as well. The versions of English that were spoken in different parts of Britain became more standardized with the invention of the printing press in about 1440. The version of English spoken by the king and in the area around London began to dominate most of Britain. The only other English dialect to survive is Scots. Poetry written after around 1500 is much easier for modern readers to understand than Middle English, though a few words have changed spelling or meaning over time. The publishing of written verses made it much easier for many poems to be preserved till the present day, usually with the poet's name recorded.

Poets found that their ability to take the time needed to compose poetry was deeply affected by political and religious events. During the lifetimes of several esteemed poets (Spenser, Shakespeare, and Donne in particular), the Protestant Reformation affected Catholic and Protestant Christians by turns during the reigns of different monarchs, putting livelihoods and even lives in danger because of religious beliefs. The English Civil War and the Commonwealth under Oliver Cromwell were challenging times. For decades, instead of writing poetry, John Milton concentrated on writing political pamphlets in support of the republican government he wanted the Commonwealth to be. The restoration of the monarchy, and later the abdication that put William and Mary of Orange on the throne, further affected the educations, employability, and livelihoods of many poets whose writing has survived to be honored as classics of English literature.

It was surprisingly difficult to earn a living as a poet; until Alexander Pope sold subscriptions for his planned translation of the *Iliad,* no one had supported himself by writing verse without writing plays as well. The financial support and social approval of a wealthy patron was needed. The most profound changes since that time for modern poets in English were first the widespread availability of affordable printing and later the development of the Internet, effectively making the costs of distributing of a poem as affordable as a loaf of bread.

The British poets discussed here are all men. Probably most of the anonymous poets were men, too. Women certainly did make and write and recite poetry, from lullabies to popular songs and even formal verse. In *The Norton Anthology of Poetry* you can find the works of Anne Askew, Queen Elizabeth I, Aphra Behn, Joanna Baillie, and eighteen other women born before 1800, among at least seventy-five men. For poetry and prose written by women, *The Norton Anthology of Literature by Women* has many celebrated works well worth reading. But women born before 1800 did not usually receive as much formal education as men, and women's use of poetry was in their homes, whether a humble cottage or a fine house, or in the seclusion of a nunnery. The poetry that was performed aloud for a wide audience, or published and distributed, was by men. It was the cultural belief of the Anglo-Saxons and for hundreds of years the English as well (unlike the British Celts they replaced) that women should not be allowed to display themselves in that way. Even in theaters and church mystery plays, until the late 1700s the female roles were all played by male actors dressed as women. Most of the writing by women published between 1600 and 1850 consisted of formal essays and travel journals, not poetry.

Of course, no one will ever know how many male poets presented the work of their wives and family members as if it were their own. It was traditional for families to work and function as a unit in many ways, whether working-class or merchants, peasants or nobles. Academic and scientific studies as well were often pursued by family members working together, as in the astronomical studies of the Herschel family. Many male poets acknowledged that they relied on at least one female family member to act as an assistant, secretary, or writing partner.

It is no surprise that, apart from anonymous folk songs by peasants, all the poetry recorded in English literature by poets born before 1800 was composed by people with at least a little education and an occupation, or by the nobility, who had wealth and leisure. Most modern readers studying these poets are doing so from a perspective of education, wealth, and leisure that was enjoyed only by the aristocracy when these poems were composed. It is now part of our cultural commonwealth that these poems are available to a literate population at large.

Notes on Rhyme and Meter

Poetry relies on several traditional techniques. Two that are of great importance for poetry written in English are the use of *meter* and *rhyme*. Meter is the measure of rhythm in poetry in patterns of syllables, with particular emphasis on the number of syllables and the accented or stressed syllables. Rhyme is from the Old French word *rime*, and the Old English word *rim*, meaning number or measure, so that in some ways rhyme is a derivative of meter or rhythm.

Poetic Meter and Rhyme

The meter of a verse is measured by the number of stressed syllables in a line. Each unit of syllables within a line is called a *foot*, which has one stressed syllable (marked with a /) and three, two, one, or no unstressed syllables (marked with a ∪). Lines lengths are labeled as follows: one foot—monometer; two feet—dimeter; three feet—trimeter; four feet—tetrameter; five feet—pentameter.

Lines of six or seven feet (hexameter or heptameter) are seen in other languages, such as French or Greek, but do not sound harmonious in English. Pentameter and tetrameter are the types most commonly seen in English poetry.

There are several common patterns for a metrical foot:

iambic (∪/) ("When in disgrace with fortune and men's eyes")

trochaic (/∪) ("Mary had a little lamb")

dactylic (/ ∪∪) ("Listen, my children, and you shall hear")

anapestic (∪∪ /) ("The Assyrian came down like a wolf on the fold")

spondee (/ /) ("top gun"; "ice cream")

Rhyme schemes are identified by assigning a letter of the alphabet to each sound at the end of a line. For example, in the nursery rhyme "Humpty Dumpty," lines one and two ("wall" and "fall") rhyme, so both of those lines are assigned the letter *a*. The next two lines end with "men" and "again." They are assigned the letter *b* because they are different from *a* but similar to each other:

Humpty Dumpty sat on a wall, *(a)*
Humpty Dumpty had a great fall. *(a)*
All the kings's horses and all the king's men *(b)*
Couldn't put Humpty Dumpty together again. *(b)*

Thus, the complete rhyme scheme is *aabb*.

The meter or rhythm of a poem is usually described as the pattern of the stressed and unstressed syllables. In English and many other modern languages, a stressed syllable is given a higher pitch or louder volume, while in languages such as Latin or Sanskrit, a syllable is emphasized by being held about twice as long as an unstressed syllable.

Rhyme is a special form of *consonance*, a technique for choosing words with sounds that are similar and harmonious together, from the Latin *con* meaning "together" and *son* meaning "sound." Consonance is also the name for selecting words by the sounds of their consonants; *assonance* is the name for selecting words by their vowel sounds. Rhyme is consonance that chooses words by their terminal sounds, such as *get* and *bet*, or *able* and *stable*. The rhyming words are usually at the end of lines of verse, but a single line can have internal rhyme when one of the words rhymes with the end word. A one-syllable rhyme (get/bet or toy/boy) is called *male rhyme*, or masculine rhyme, while a rhyme with more than one syllable (able/stable or intentional/dimensional) is called *female rhyme*, or feminine rhyme. In English, female rhyme is nearly always used for humor.

These examples are all full rhymes, or "perfect" rhymes. Other forms of rhyme include *rime riche*, in which the rhyming words sound identical (maid/made), *slant rhyme*, in which the consonants are the same but the vowels different (love/have), and *eye rhyme*, where the words have matching spelling but not sounds (through/rough).

Rhyme is not commonly used in many languages, and it was not important in British poetry until about the fourteenth century, when it began to replace *alliteration*, the repetition of initial sounds of words. Both alliteration and rhyme are seen in the slogan from the Second World War "Loose lips sink ships": the alliteration of *l* sounds and *s* sounds, and the rhyme of *lips* and *ships*. An interesting discussion of rhyme and rhythm occurs in Isak Dinesen's memoir *Out of Africa*, when she improvised poetry in Swahili in simple quatrains (four-lined verses, usually iambic or trochaic, with male end rhyme on the second and fourth lines in an *abcb* pattern).

Anglo-Saxon Poets

(approx. 600–1000)

Poets were highly respected both by the Anglo-Saxons and by the Celts, who lived before them in Britain. We who use modern English have newspapers, radio, and television for sharing the news, and libraries full of books about recent and past events. We talk with each other over long distances by telephone and the Internet, and many of us routinely travel to distant places, too. Life was not like that for the people who spoke Old English. A journey of five hundred miles was very long indeed.

Instead of books and modern media, the Anglo-Saxon people relied on the oral memory of a poet, or *scop* (pronounced "skope"). The word *scop* was related to the word *scleppan* (to shape or create), and to *scleppend* (shaper, creator, and God), just as the modern English word *poet* is derived from a word in ancient Greek that means potter, shaper, creator, and God. Scops chanted memorized poems about past events and invented new verses about new events, both trivial and of historical importance, much like the Celtic bards before them. Sometimes a scop would be supported by a local chieftain, but some scops traveled from place to place bringing new stories.

One of the traditions of an Anglo-Saxon dining hall was that a cup would be passed from hand to hand, and each person would call out a toast before drinking. A harp would be passed around as well, and each person would take a turn singing a song—not as well as a scop, but each taking a fair turn. There might be group songs, riddles, traditional chants, and homemade doggerel.

There is no way to know how many poets were working in Britain at that time. The few surviving poems were all copied by monks after the Anglo-Saxon tribes largely converted to Christianity around the year 600 C.E. Only four books containing poetry have been preserved.

Ray Winstone as the hero in the 2007 movie version of *Beowulf*. This Anglo-Saxon saga has fascinated readers for centuries.

The Ruin

Well-wrought this wall: Wierds broke it,
The stronghold burst …
Snapped rooftrees, towers fallen,
the work of the Giants, the stonesmiths,
mouldereth.

      Rime scoureth gatetowers
      rime on mortar.

Shattered the showershields, roofs ruined,
age under-ate them.

      And the wielders & wrights?
Earthgrip holds them—gone, long gone,
Fast in gravesgrasp while fifty fathers
and sons have passed.

      Wall stood,
grey lichen, red stone, kings fell often,
stood under storms, high arch crashed—
stands yet the wallstone, hacked by weapons,
by files grim-ground …
… shone the old skilled work
… sank to loam-crust.

Mood quickened mind, and a man of wit,
cunning in rings, bound bravely the wallbase
with iron, a wonder.

Bright were the buildings, halls where springs ran,
high, horngabled, much throng-noise;
these many meadhalls men filled
with loud cheerfulness: Wierd changed that.

Came days of pestilence, on all sides men fell dead,
death fetched off the flower of the people;
where they stood to fight, waste places
and on the acropolis, ruins.

       Hosts who would build again
shrank to the earth. Therefore are these courts dreary
and that red arch twisteth tiles,
wryeth from roof-ridge, reacheth groundswards....
Broken blocks ...
       There once many a man
mood-glad, goldbright, of gleams garnished,
flushed with wine-pride, flashing war-gear,
gazed on wrought gemstones, on gold, on silver,
on wealth held and hoarded, on light-filled amber,
on this bright burg of broad dominion.

Stood stone houses: wide streams welled
hot from source, and a wall all caught
in its bright bosom, that the baths were
hot at hall's hearth; that was fitting ...
...
Thence hot streams, loosed, ran over hoar stone
unto the ring-tank ...
... it is a kingly thing
... city ...

Wierds—the translator's spelling of Wyrds, or Fates. See Themes, below.
rime—frost
wryeth—twists or wrenches

Summary and ExpLication

The anonymous poet is looking at the ruins of Aquae Sulis, built by the Romans seven hundred years earlier, at the hot springs near the modern city of Bath in England. Where there are ellipsis points (…), there are words missing because the page was burned.

This strong wall and buildings were broken by the Fates. The people who made it were as strong as giants, but they died fifty generations ago. Lichen has grown on the stones of the wall that kings died defending. The arch has fallen, but the wall's good stonework still shows, though damaged.

A genius who knew how to make wealth and share it used iron bands to strengthen the wall. The buildings over the hot springs had high roofs with antlers on the gables, and the halls where men drank mead were filled with noisy, cheerful crowds. Fate changed that. Disease came and people died, leaving empty, unused land where they fought and ruins on the city hill.

People who built there again eventually died, and their renovations crumbled. There used to be many men there, happy and drunk, wearing gold and weapons, looking at their wealth of money and this city. Stone houses were built so the hot springs were inside the wall and hall. This was a city fit for kings.

Poetic Techniques

Poetry in Old English does not count the number of words or syllables. Each line has instead four stressed syllables, with a pause (called a *caesura*) after the first two. Sentences usually begin after this midline pause, which may have been emphasized by the poet striking a chord on a harp.

Instead of rhyming the end of words, the poets used alliteration—selecting words by the first sound. The first stress after a mid-line pause sets the sound for the alliteration. Of the two stresses in the first half-line, one must alliterate with it, and the other may. But the last stress must not alliterate with it. When translated into modern English, the alliteration sometimes disappears, but it still shows in the lines:

*fl*ushed with wine-pride, || *fl*ashing war-gear,
*g*azed on wrought *g*emstones, || on *g*old, on *s*ilver,

This pattern of four stressed syllables per line, often arranged as alternating stressed and unstressed syllables, survives today in folk songs, ballads, country and western songs, and even the eight-bar blues, where songs have repeating patterns of four or eight guitar strums or bars of written music.

Compound words not only provide a strong visual image but also use the meaning of both words where a plainer, common word would have served: rooftree, showershields, gravesgrasp, horngabled, throng-noise, mood-glad, goldbright, wine-pride. Compound words may not have been used much in

Caedmon

About 658 c.e., an illiterate herdsman named Caedmon employed by the monastery of Whitby would slink out of the hall after dinner when the harp came his way. One night he hid in the stable, where a man appeared to him in a dream and asked him to sing. When he protested that he did not know how, the man insisted he sing of the Creation. Caedmon began singing well-shaped verses in a clear, pleasing voice that carried to the astonished monks. After testing, they regarded his gift as a miracle; but it is possible Caedmon had concealed some training as a scop in pagan poetry. He became a lay brother, a member of the monastery without formal vows as a full monk, and he founded a school of Christian poetry. After his vision, he could compose fine verses based on any religious story that someone told or read to him.[1]

casual speech, but they are common in Anglo-Saxon verse. Some of these compound words were stock epithets, such as "swan's-road" for the sea, used as Homer used stock epithets in the *Iliad* and the *Odyssey*, as an aid to memory and also a reference to earlier verses and poems.

Themes

There are references to Wierd or Wierds, the translator's spelling of the Anglo-Saxon *Wyrd* and *Wyrds*, Fate and the goddesses of Fate. These goddesses appear throughout European religions as arbiters of human lives and are often considered to end human lives abruptly as an example of their power. The word *Wyrd* has come into modern English as "weird."

The horngabled halls have antlers displayed, not only as hunting trophies but also as an homage to pagan gods from Norse and Celtic traditions. Though the writers who recorded the poem were definitely Christian monks, the poet is showing his Norse traditions.

The poet was clearly in awe of the stonework. None like it had been constructed for over six hundred years, nor would any be for another three hundred or more. To the Anglo-Saxons, these Roman ruins were manifestly the work of giants.

Commentary

An ordinary conversation in Old English would not have been full of alliteration, nor so many compound words. "In a primitive society the poet is historian and priest, and his songs have ritual significance," Michael Alexander says in his translation into modern language of *The Earliest English Poems*. "That is why the language of the poets was so deeply conservative, and why the written records of it that we have show it so different from the language of the earliest prose-writers."[2] This trend for formal poetic language being more old-fashioned and structured than prose or casual speech has lingered until the present day in modern English. It even has an influence upon the most trivial of popular songs, as discussed openly in the song "Hook" by Blues Traveler.

Wulf and Eadwacer

The men of my tribe would treat him as game:
if he comes on the camp they will kill him outright.

   Our fate is forked.

Wulf is on one island, I on another.
Mine is a fastness: the fens girdle it
and it is defended by the fiercest men.
If he comes to the camp they will kill him for sure.

   Our fate is forked.

It was rainy weather, and I wept by the hearth,
thinking of my Wulf's far wanderings;
one of the captains caught me in his arms.
It gladdened me then; but it grieved me too.

Wulf, my Wulf, it was wanting you
that made me sick, your seldom coming,
the hollowness at heart; not the hunger I spoke of.

Do you hear, Eadwacer? Our whelp
      Wulf shall take to the wood.
What was never bound is broken easily,
      our song together.

fens—bogs

whelp—wolf pup

Summary and Explication

This poem is notoriously difficult to interpret. Most critics believe the speaker is an unnamed woman, guarded on one island while Wulf is on another. But is she a prisoner or a queen? Is Wulf her lover or her son? And if either, why is he the enemy of her defenders? Is Eadwacer her husband or the captain who caught her in his arms? Is Wulf their son, or will he steal their child to raise as a wolf's head (outlaw) in the wilderness?

Gnomish Riddle 30

I am fire-fretted and I flirt with Wind
and my limbs are light-freighted and I am lapped in flame
and I am storm-stacked and I strain to fly
and I am a grove leaf-bearing and a glowing ember.

From hand to friend's hand about the hall I go,
so much do lords and ladies love to kiss me.
When I hold myself high, and the whole company
bow quiet before me, their blessedness
shall flourish skyward beneath my fostering shade.

Summary and Explication

The solution for this riddle is wood, or in Old English *beam*, which the translator Michael Alexander advises can mean tree, or any of several things carved from wood, such as the series here of log, ship, harp, cup, or cross.

Critical Response To Anglo-Saxon Poetry

It is hard to make a detailed, useful, and accurate criticism of a branch of poetry represented only by four books. "There is no reason to suppose, either, that what Time has spared is necessarily the best," Alexander points out.[3] The chief of these miscellaneous collections, the Exeter book, survived over a thousand years but is damaged. "The front has been used as a cutting-board and, more appropriately, as a beer mat," says Alexander, while "the back fourteen pages have been burnt through by a brand."[4] He admits that "Anglo-Saxon will never be considered one of the great literatures of the world."[5]

Alexander Pope considered Anglo-Saxon poetry to be dull, especially compared with the *Iliad* and the *Odyssey* by Homer, but as oral poetry recited aloud to keep a community's memory and heritage alive, it was closer to Homer than to Pope's satires. Far from being dull to modern writers, Anglo-Saxon verse (and particularly the epic poem *Beowulf*) has inspired the creation of no less than four films in the last fifteen years, including one released in 2007.

Suggested Further Reading

Dungeons and Dragons and other role-playing games owe a great deal to *Beowulf*, the most famous of all Anglo-Saxon poems. The best translations of *Beowulf* are by J.R.R. Tolkien (author of *The Hobbit* and *The Lord of the Rings*) and more recently by Seamus Heaney. Tolkien also wrote *The Homecoming of Beorhtnoth Beorthelm's Son*, about a boy and an old man after the Battle of Maldon. After reading *Beowulf*, read the novel *Grendel* by John Gardner to see the monster's point of view.

2

Geoffrey Chaucer

(c. 1342–1400)

Geoffrey Chaucer was born in London sometime before 1343, the son of John Chaucer, a wine importer, and his wife, Agnes. As the son and grandson of men in public office, young Geoffrey was raised in a well-to-do family with connections to the royal court and the Lancastrian court. Their name meant both "hunter" and "shoemaker" in French. At about age fourteen, he became a page in the household of Prince Lionel, second son of King Edward III, beginning his education as a courtier.

Chaucer served with the English army in France in 1359 and 1360, was taken prisoner at the Siege of Reims and ransomed, and became a courier for Prince Lionel during peace negotiations. As a royal esquire, he served as a government official in civil service. He studied law and finance and traveled to Ireland and Spain with the army. Visiting Italy and France several times from 1372 to 1377, Chaucer negotiated treaties and was introduced to the Italian culture of Dante, Petrarch, and Boccaccio during the early period of Renaissance humanism.

As Comptroller of the King's Custom and Subsidy of wools, skins and hides in the port of London; Comptroller of the Petty Customs on wine and other merchandise; Justice of the Peace in Kent; and later, under King Richard II, Clerk of the King's Works, he was a responsible civil servant and public official.

His marriage to Philippa Roet in 1366 produced three or four children. After a long and active life, Chaucer died on October 25, 1400, and was buried in Westminster Abbey. During the English Renaissance, the area around his tomb grew in significance as Poets' Corner, where a succession of honored poets were buried.

Two panels of a mural from the U.S. Library of Congress show illustrations by Ezra Winter from Chaucer's *Canterbury Tales*.

Truth

Flee fro the prees and dwelle with soothfastnesse,
Suffyce unto thy good, though hit be small;
For hoord hath hate, and climbing tikelnesse,
Prees hath envye, and wele blent overall.
Savour no more than thee bihove shal;
Werk wel thy-self, that other folk canst rede.
And trouthe shal delivere, hit is no drede.

Tempest thee noght al croked to redresse
In trust of hir that turneth as a bal:
Gret reste stant in litel besinesse;
And eek be war therefore to sporne ageyn an al;
Stryve noght, as dooth the crokke with the wal.
Daunte thy-self, that dauntest otheres dede:
And trouthe shal delivere, hit is no drede.

That thee is sent, receyve in buxomnesse;
The wrastling for the world axeth a fal;
Her is non hoom, here nis but wilderness:
Forth, pilgrim, forth! Forth beste, out of thy stal!
Know thy contree, look up, thank God of al.
Hold the hye wey, and lat thy gost thee lede:
And trouthe shal delivere, it is no drede.

Therefore, thou vache, leve thyn old wrecchednesse
Unto the worlde; leve now to be thrall;
Crye him mercy, that of his hy goodnesse
Made thee of noght, and in especial
Draw unto him, and pray in general,
For thee, and eek for other, hevenelich meede;
And trouthe shal delivere, hit is no drede.

Summary and Explication

The poet is giving advice to his friend Sir Philip de la Vache:

> Flee from crowds, and live honestly.
> Be satisfied with what little you have,
> for hoarding causes hate, and coveting makes you insecure.
> Pricey possessions cause envy, and prosperity makes you blind.
> Do not get hungry for more than you need.
> Control yourself and set a good example for others.
> Truth shall set you free, no doubt.
>
> Do not worry about straightening everything that is crooked.
> Fortune turns like a ball, turning a different face wherever you look.
> Peace of mind stands in little anxiety (rest easy without fussing);
> be wary of kicking against a sharp awl.
> Do not fight and break like a pot against a wall.
> Be your own master, and a good example.
> Take to heart what you are given;
> wrestling for worldly success is asking for a fall.
> There is no home here, nothing but wilderness.
> Go out on a spiritual quest. Do not stay indoors like a cow in a barn.
> Know your country, look up, thank the God of everything.
> Keep on the right path and let your spirit lead you.
> So, you cow, leave your old wretchedness
> to the world; do not be a slave.
> Ask for God's mercy,
> and pray for yourself and others.
> That is as right as a heavenly meadow.

Poetic Techniques

These verses are written in iambic pentameter. In this pattern, there are five stressed syllables in each line, and each stressed syllable (/) usually follows an unstressed syllable (∪). That pattern ∪ / is one meter, or foot—one measurement of syllables in the line. This pattern is named an iamb, one iambic meter. When there are five meters in a line, the pattern is called pentameter (*penta* means five in Latin):

∪　∕　∪　∕　∪　　　∕　　∪　　∕∪　　∕
Suffyce unto thy good, though hit be small

The unstressed syllable and the stressed syllable do not have to be in the same word. In iambic pentameter, not all the lines will be perfect. There may be an extra unstressed syllable or two in some lines, or the ∪ ∕ may be reversed to ∕ ∪ once in a while. For particular emphasis, there may be two or three stressed syllables in a row. This pattern of usually alternating an unstressed and a stressed syllable is very much like ordinary speech in modern English. It allows the poem to be read aloud in a natural way.

The last syllables of these lines rhyme in the pattern *ababbcc*, so that the first line rhymes with the third, the second with the fourth and fifth, and the verse ends with a couplet, a pair of rhymed lines, which makes the thought seem complete and finished. The final line of each verse is identical, a technique common to both cautionary (warning) verses and entertainments. This poem was probably intended as both.

The verses are more than just a list of what to avoid and what to do. "Axeth a fal" refers to the Biblical proverb "Pride goes before a fall," which was old in Chaucer's day. "Fall" here is a pun on both a fall in a wrestling bout and the biblical Fall of Man through sin. The poem ends with a pun on "meede," which means both meet (right) and reward, and also meadow.

FACTS

Chaucer and two London merchants were charged with rape, but plaintiff Cecily Champain formally released them all from any legal action in 1380. It seems to have been a civil case of abduction, not a criminal case of sexual assault, and details are vague. One interpretation is that Chaucer helped his friend's fiancée to elope against her father's wishes.

Themes

The word *truth* had three meanings here: the real world, religious truth, and the moral virtue of integrity. "By maintaining one's faith and one's integrity," says E. Talbot Donaldson in the *Norton Anthology of English Literature*, "one rises superior to the vicissitudes of this world and comes eventually to know reality."[1] As Christ advised his disciples in John 8:32, "And ye shall know the truth, and the truth shall make you free."

Morality was of great interest in Chaucer's time. The plague arrived in England in 1348 and returned five times before the end of the century. The Black Death killed a third or more of all the people in Europe—many English villages saw half their people die, and some two hundred thousand villages were wiped out across Europe. Many survivors prayed obsessively, others drank and lusted, but all feared a very present death. As Catholics, most people believed that at death they would face God's judgment for their sins, so morality and repentance were on everyone's minds.

Commentary

This is not a grim reminder as Chaucer tells his friend to clean up his act; it is more like Polonius's speech to Laertes in Shakespeare's play *Hamlet* (act 1, scene 3). There are puns and proverbs showing a sense of humor here.

Though Chaucer did not read Anglo-Saxon verse, these lines in places read like Anglo-Saxon gnomic verses or riddles. ("For hoord hath hate, and climbing tikelnesse / Prees hath envye, and wele blent overall.") While Chaucer was growing up, educated people in England spoke French as well as English. Both languages were changing in vocabulary and pronunciation, and during his lifetime the bias shifted to promote English. Chaucer used the best words available, conservatively, borrowing poetic forms from French poetry because that was the literature available. Much contemporary Middle English poetry seemed dull and uncouth to him. Simply by writing in the way he was speaking, in the language of commerce and daily interactions, Chaucer created a body of work that interested many people.

To His Scribe Adam

Adam scriveyn, if evere it thee bifalle
Boece or Troilus *to wryten newe,*
Under thy lokkes thou most have the scalle,
But after my making thou wryte more trewe
So ofte a daye I mot thy werk renewe,
Hit to correcte, and eek to rubbe and scrape;
And al is through thy negligence and rape.

Summary

The poet addresses his writing assistant, Adam, saying: If you ever have to make a new copy of the work by the Italian poet Boece I'm translating or my play *Troilus*, I hope you get a scabby, itchy scalp disease under your long hair. When I make you do a true copy, most days I have to fix your work, correct errors, and even erase places, all because of your negligence and haste.

Critical Response To Chaucer

Chaucer was recognized as a major poet, translator, and writer of rhetoric during his lifetime. There were other writers and poets in his day, but Chaucer's poetry has come to be regarded as among the earliest literature in English.

Handmade copies of his works were popular among educated people, and printed copies later, for hundreds of years. He was read more than imitated during the Renaissance; Reformation poets thought of him as an early Reformer or Protestant (though he was definitely a Catholic). During the Restoration and eighteenth century, he was considered refreshingly simple and naïve. By the twentieth century, he was interpreted as an ironic social commentator with a "'naïve narrator' created as a mouthpiece,"[2] according to Donald Howard.

Merciles Beaute: A Triple Roundel

I. Captivity

Your eyen two wol slee me sodenly,
I may the beautè of hem not sustene,
So woundeth hit through-out my herte kene.
And but your word wol helen hastily
My hertes wounde, whyl that hit is grene,
    Your eyen two wol slee me sodenly,
    I may the beautè of hem not sustene.

Upon my trouthe I sey yow feithfully
That ye ben of my lyf and deeth the quene;
For with my deeth the trouthe shal be sene.
    Your eyen two wol slee me sodenly
    I may the beautè of hem not sustene,
    So woundeth hit through-out my herte kene.

II. Rejection

So hath your beautè fro your herte chaced
Pitee, that me ne availeth not to pleyne;
For Daunger halt your mercy in his cheyne.

Giltles my deeth thus han ye me purchaced;
I sey yow sooth, me nedeth not to feyne;
    So hath your beautè fro your herte chaced
    Pitee, that me ne availeth not to pleyne.

Allas! that Nature hath in yow compassed
So greet beautè, that no man may atteyne
To mercy, though he sterve for the peyne.

So hath your beautè fro your herte chaced
Pitee, that me ne availeth not to pleyne;
For Daunger halt your mercy in his cheyne.

III. Escape

Sin I fro Love escaped am so fat,
I never thenk to ben in his prison lene;
Sin I am free, I counte him not a bene.

He may answere, and seye this and that;
I do no fors, I speke right as I mene.
    Sin I fro Love escaped am so fat
    I never thenk to ben in his prison lene.

Love hath my name y-strike out of his sclat,
And he is strike out of my bokes clene
For ever-mo; ther is non other mene.
    Sin I fro Love escaped am so fat,
    I never thenk to ben in his prison lene;
    Sin I am free, I counte him not a bene.

eyen—eyes

helen—heal

pleyne—complain

feyne—feign (pretend)

Sin I fro Love escaped am so fat—Since I have escaped so healthy from Love

ben—being

bene—bean

fors—force (as in try to make up a false answer)

sclat—slate (piece of flat stone for erasable writing with a graphite pencil or chalk)

Thomas Gray suggested about 1760 that Chaucer's writing is easier for modern readers when every syllable is pronounced, even the *e* at the end of many words. Consonants that modern speakers leave silent in many words—such as *folk, gnat,* or *knight*—were pronounced. During the fifteenth century, as the language was changing, critics were not aware of the process. Chaucer was still admired, but his narrative power was considered stronger than his verses, which seemed clumsy with rough rhymes. The language changes were slower in Scotland, where Chaucer's poetry had potent influence. When the progressive language changes were recognized, Chaucer's posthumous reputation was much improved. No one is sure exactly how fourteenth-century English sounded. Some literature professors read Middle English aloud in a thick Scots brogue with a breathy soft "ah" sound where a letter *e* appears at the end of many words; others pronounce Middle English like Low German.

Suggested Further Reading

An enjoyable reference Web site is *Geoffrey Chaucer Online: The Electronic Canterbury Tales.* Any detailed biography of Chaucer will bring up fascinating facts about how England was governed under Edward III, Richard II, and Henry IV. For insight into the minds of literary women of Chaucer's time, look to the writings of Julian of Norwich, an abbess and educated woman.

3

Anonymous Folk Songs
(c. 1100–1600)

Traditional folk songs and ballads were handed down orally, sometimes for hundreds of years. Ballads and folk songs were sung by peasants and the common people of small towns, people singing simply and informally about things they had seen and heard. These are not formal verses like those Celtic bards used to chant before Roman times and scops would chant in Anglo-Saxon halls, or the literary, romantic songs of French minstrels heard by travelers and Crusaders.

Some critics believe that folk songs began as popular and fashionable songs originally composed by individuals, like most poetry, and handed down orally, with errors accumulating. The anonymous author has been forgotten. Certainly there were ballads published cheaply as "broadsides" or broadsheets, a single sheet of paper printed on one side. As the production of paper increased, literacy increased, and these broadsides were sold at fairs, on street corners, and by peddlers. This was the equivalent of newspaper columnists and modern talk shows on television and radio.

Other scholars are more impressed by the natural spontaneous and unconventional qualities of folk songs and insist that this is because the songs are composed not so much by an individual as by a succession of singers engaging in a dialogue with the song and its subject. Oral tradition therefore not only preserves but also molds and develops the song. The anonymous author has become part of a community practicing its culture. As Ursula K. Le Guin observes in her novel *Always Coming Home*, "a song is its singing."

Clothing and Literacy

For over a thousand years, clothing for a rural peasant was simple: a tunic or dress, with perhaps a smock or trousers in the cold. People migrating from rural to urban areas in the thirteenth century began with increasing frequency to wear undergarments instead of just a tunic. This actually had an effect on literacy, as papermakers used rags from worn-out linen undergarments to make paper. The increased production of paper made books more common and affordable than parchment had ever been. The availability of something to read after about 1200 caused literacy to become increasingly a skill practiced by some working people as well as the clergy and nobles.

Lord Randal

"O where ha' you been, Lord Randal, my son?
And where ha' you been, my handsome young man?"
"I ha' been at the greenwood; mother, mak my bed soon,
For I'm wearied wi' huntin', and I fain wad lie down."

"And wha met ye there, Lord Randal my son?
And wha met you there, my handsome young man?"
"O I met wi' my true-love; mother, mak my bed soon,
For I'm wearied wi' huntin', and I fain wad lie down."

"And what did she give you, Lord Randal, my son?
And what did she give you, my handsome young man?"
"Eels fried in a pan; mother, mak my bed soon,
For I'm wearied wi' huntin', and I fain wad lie down."

"And wha gat your leavin's, Lord Randal, my son?
And wha gat your leavin's, my handsome young man?"
"My hawks and my hounds; mother, mak my bed soon,
For I'm wearied wi' huntin', and I fain wad lie down."

"And what becam of them, Lord Randal, my son?
And what becam of them, my handsome young man?"
"They stretched their legs out and died; mother, mak my bed
soon,
For I'm wearied wi' huntin', and I fain wad lie down."

"O I fear you are poisoned, Lord Randal, my son!
I fear you are poisoned, my handsome young man!"
"O yes, I am poisoned; mother, mak my bed soon,
For I'm sick at the heart, and I fain wad lie down."

"What d'ye leave to your mother, Lord Randal, my son?
What d'ye leave to your mother, my handsome young man?"
"Four and twenty milk kye; mother, mak my bed soon,
For I'm sick at the heart, and I fain wad lie down."

"What d'ye leave to your sister, Lord Randal, my son?
What d'ye leave to your sister, my handsome young man?"
"My gold and my silver; mother, mak my bed soon,
For I'm sick at the heart, and I fain wad lie down."

"What d'ye leave to your brother, Lord Randal, my son?
What d'ye leave to your brother, my handsome young man?"
"My houses and my lands; mother, mak my bed soon,
For I'm sick at the heart, and I fain wad lie down."

"What d'ye leave to your true-love, Lord Randal, my son?
What d'ye leave to your true-love, my handsome young man?"
"I leave her hell and fire; mother, mak my bed soon,
For I'm sick at the heart, and I fain wad lie down."

fain—truly intend (fain wad lie down = really would rather lie down)

kye—cattle (milk kye = dairy cows)

Summary and Explication

The ballad is sung as a dialogue between a mother and her son. She asks where he has been. He tells her he has been in the woods, and he asks her to make his bed, for he is tired from hunting and wants to lie down. Answering her questions, he tells her he met with his true love, who gave him eels fried in a pan. His hunting birds and dogs ate the leftovers and died. His mother fears he has been poisoned, and he agrees, brokenhearted and in pain. He makes his will, leaving his twenty-four milk cows to his mother, gold and silver to his sister, and houses and lands to his brother. He expects his true love to go to hell for poisoning him.

Poetic Techniques

These verses are made in an "answer song" pattern. It is possible that one singer would sing the words that change with each verse, and the rest of a group of singers would sing the words that remain the same. Alternatively, one singer could sing the part of the mother and another singer the role of her son.

The progressive verses are a standard pattern in many traditional songs, like the popular Christmas carol "The Twelve Days of Christmas." In this ballad, the progressive verses detail the son leaving all his property to various members of his family. It is easy to imagine that over time a number of changes might slip into the song at this point in particular, if the singer confuses two verses or wishes to extend the song or shorten it for various performances.

Themes

The meal of "eels fried in a pan" is not an unreasonable one. Many people did and do eat fried fish or eels, perhaps cooked over a campfire in the woods. But the inference is that Randal's true love has fed him snakes, which were widely believed to be poisonous. This erroneous belief was due at least in part to the Bible story in Genesis of the serpent that enticed Eve to eat the forbidden fruit, which granted knowledge of good and evil. In other versions of the ballad, the poison in the dish is supposed to be toads.

Commentary

This ballad is found throughout Great Britain from Scotland to Cornwall, and in Ireland as well as Denmark, Sweden, Iceland, Italy, Germany, Holland, and Hungary. It is discussed thoroughly by the famous folklorist F. J. Child, as Number 12A in his collection of English and Scottish ballads, which he researched exhaustively and published in five volumes from 1882 to 1898.

Sir Walter Scott believed the ballad originally referred to Thomas Randolph or Randal, Earl of Murray. This man was governor of Scotland and nephew to

A painting by the famous illustrator Arthur Rackham shows Lord Randal dining on poisoned eels, with his murderous love at his side.

Robert Bruce; he died at Musselburgh in 1332. Because he was sorely needed by his country, historians assumed his untimely death was no accident, but a convenient assassination done by poison. Perhaps an older story and song were adapted to suit that name and time.

A modern song that draws heavily upon "Lord Randal" is Bob Dylan's song "A Hard Rain's A-Gonna Fall," with opening lines that paraphrase those of the ballad. A modern "answer song" ballad is Stan Rogers's "Barrett's Privateers"; recordings show that sometimes these ballads were enjoyed as a group song rather than a solo performance.

CriTicaL Response To TradiTionaL FoLk Songs

Until almost the end of the nineteenth century, there was little formal or literary knowledge of traditional English ballads and folk songs. The songs that were still being sung in a few isolated places had been carefully ignored by English literary critics since before the Renaissance. All the efforts of formal poets went to bringing a grand quality to English verse like that of Italy and France. Dante was admired; doggerel was ignored by critics. Sometimes a popular song would be sung between the acts of a play, as a crowd-pleaser. Cecil Sharp wrote in *One Hundred English Folksongs*:

> The knowledge that folksongs existed in this country was confined to very few. It was popularly assumed that the English peasant was the only one of his class in Europe who had failed to express himself spontaneously in song and dance.... With the passing of the last survivors of the peasant class ... the products of a great peasant art would have been irrevocably lost.[1]

While Sir Walter Scott had collected some songs in his *Minstrelsy of the Scottish Border* (1828), and others privately distributed small collections, the most famous collector of ballads was F. J. Child. Thus began the modern recognition by the literate public that traditional English folk songs existed and were of interest to more than just a few literary academics.

Barbara Allan

It was in and about the Martinmas time,
When the green leaves were a falling,
That Sir John Graeme, in the West Country,
Fell in love with Barbara Allan.

He sent his man down through the town,
To the place where she was dwelling,
"O haste and come to my master dear,
Gin ye be Barbara Allan."

O hooly, hooly rose she up,
To the place where he was lying,
And when she drew the curtain by,
"Young man, I think you're dying."

"O it's I'm sick, and very, very sick,
And 'tis a' for Barbara Allan."
"O the better for me ye's never be,
Though your heart's blood were aspilling."

"O dinna ye mind, young man," said she,
"When ye was in the tavern adrinking,
That ye made the healths gae round and round,
And slighted Barbara Allan?"

He turned his face unto the wall,
And death was with him dealing.
"Adieu, adieu, my dear friends all,
And be kind to Barbara Allan."

And slowly, slowly raise she up,
And slowly, slowly left him,
And sighing said, she could not stay.
Since death of life had reft him.

She had not gane a mile but twa,
When she heard the dead-bell ringing,
And every jow that dead-bell gied,
It cry'd, Woe to Barbara Allan!

"O mother, mother, make my bed!
O make it saft and narrow!
Since my love died for me today,
I'll die for him to-morrow."

Martinmas—the feast of St. Martin, November 11

gin—if

hooly—slowly

dinna ye mind—do you not remember

jow—toll (ringing sound)

Jolly Good Ale and Old

I cannot eat but little meat,
My stomach is not good;
But sure I think that I can drink
With him that wears a hood.
Though I go bare, take ye no care,
I nothing am a-cold;
I stuff my skin so full within
Of jolly good ale and old.

Back and side go bare, go bare,
Both foot and hand go cold;
But, belly, God send thee good ale enough,
Whether it be new or old.

I love no roast but a nut-brown toast,
And a crab laid in the fire;
A little bread shall do me stead,
Much bread I not desire.
No frost nor snow, no wind, I trow,
Can hurt me if I wold,
I am so wrapp'd, and thoroughly lapp'd
Of jolly good ale and old.

Back and side go bare, go bare,
Both foot and hand go cold;
But, belly, God send thee good ale enough,
Whether it be new or old.

crab—crab apple

A woodcut illustrating the Roxburghe Ballad book shows men
drinking ale in a tavern. A number of folk songs celebrate
drinking and revelry.

Suggested Further Reading

F. J. Child's *English and Scottish Popular Ballads* (1882–1898) is still a useful
reference. For understanding the lives of people who sang these songs, try Roy
Palmer's book *The Painful Plough* and Cecil Sharp's *One Hundred English
Folksongs*.

There are several modern poets working in the ballad form. Songwriters Pete
Seeger, Gordon Lightfoot, and Billy Bragg acknowledge their debts to traditional
English ballads. Dudley Randall's "Ballad of Birmingham" and Richard Fariña's
"Birmingham Sunday" both borrow patterns from the ballads "Tam Lin" and
"The Douglas Tragedy" to tell of the bombing of a church in Birmingham,
Alabama, in 1963, during the civil rights marches.

4

Sir Edmund Spenser

(1552–1599)

Edmund Spenser was born in or near 1552 in East Smithfield in London, probably the son of John Spenser, a clothmaker originally from Lancashire. When the Merchant Taylors' school opened in 1561, young Edmund was a student supported by warden Nicholas Spenser and Robert Nowell. There he studied the Roman classics and some Greek and Hebrew works, and he was encouraged by the masters to write verse.

Spenser went to Pembroke Hall, Cambridge, in 1569 with a small bequest from Nowell and worked there for his meals and accommodation. His studies there led to friendships with future bishops and men of influence. After completing his bachelor's degree (1573) and master's degree (1576), Spenser worked in Kent as secretary for his former teacher John Young, newly made the Bishop of Rochester. There he wrote *The Shepheardes Calender*, printed in 1579.

He then worked for the Earl of Leicester in London, becoming acquainted with other artistic young men in an intellectual society informally called the "Areopagus." Two short books soon appeared from a well-known printer, collecting letters between Spenser and his school friend Gabriel Harvey discussing trendy intellectual matters of law, philosophy, and poetry.

In 1580, Spenser went to Ireland as secretary to Lord Grey de Wilton, the new Lord Deputy of Ireland. Lord Grey's forces marched from Dublin to Munster, where they defeated papal and Spanish forces. Spenser was granted an estate and civil service duties in Munster, and there met Sir Walter Raleigh. Impressed with Spenser's poetry, Raleigh brought him to London in 1590 and presented Spenser to Queen Elizabeth I.

While in London, Spenser published the first three books of *The Faerie Queene*. Although the queen promised him a pension, Lord Burghley interceded and moderated her generosity. Spenser wrote *Complaints* to lampoon Burghley in 1591, and the work was suppressed almost immediately. Wisely returning to his Irish residence, Spenser soon met and courted Elizabeth Boyle. They were married in 1594. His works celebrating their love—*Amoretti,* a sonnet cycle, and *Epithalamion*, a long poem—were published in one volume a year later.

In 1596, Spenser visited London for almost a year, seeing the last three books of *The Faerie Queene* and some shorter works published and working on a treatise on the social and political reformation of Ireland. Without court favors, he returned to Ireland by early 1598. He was appointed sSheriff for County Cork, but before the year ended, rebellion in Munster caused Spenser and his family to flee to the city of Cork for safety.

Spenser was sent to London with messages for the Privy Council, and died there January 16, 1599. Poet Ben Johnson attributed his death to a lack of bread, a puzzling fate for a politically well-connected official and a well-loved poet. The Earl of Essex paid for his funeral, and poets carried his coffin, throwing their verses and pens into his grave beside that of Chaucer in Westminster Abbey.

Sonnet 75
from Amoretti

One day I wrote her name upon the strand,
But came the waves and washed it away;
Agayne I wrote it with a second hand;
But came the tyde, and made my paynes his pray.
"Vayne man," sayd she, "that doest in vaine assay
A mortall thing so to immortalize;
For I my selve shall lyke to this decay,
And eek my name bee wiped out lykewize."
"Not so," quod I; "let baser things devize
To dy in dust, but you shall live by fame:
My verse your vertues rare shall eternize,
And in the hevens wryte your glorious name.
Where, when as death shall all the world subdew,
Our love shall live, and later life renew."

assay—try

eek—also

Summary and Explication

Spenser is telling about a time when he wrote in the sand the name of the woman he loved. The waves washed it away, even when he tried again. The woman called him proud, saying it was useless to try to make her name last, for she would die one day and her name be forgotten. But he disagreed. Let ordinary things plan to die in dust, he said. She would be famous forever. His poem would make her rare virtues last forever and write her name in heaven. When death conquers the whole world, their love would still exist and bring new life.

Poetic Techniques

This poem is written in a sonnet format, an English version of sonnets ("little songs") made popular in Italian by the poet Petrarch. Each line has a pattern of stressed and unstressed syllables called iambic pentameter.

The rhyme scheme in this sonnet is *abab acac cdcd ee*. There are different rhyme schemes for sonnets written by Spenser, Shakespeare, Donne, Milton, or Elizabeth Barrett Browning. But all sonnets have fourteen lines, and all are written in iambic pentameter. The lines are arranged so that the first eight lines (called an octave) usually complete one thought, and the final six lines (called a sestet) complete a contrasting or complementary thought. The interest for writing sonnets in English began as a passionate admiration of Italian culture and lingers to the twenty-first century.

Themes

Sonnets are often written about a moment of understanding. This moment can be about emotions, intellect, or both, as in this poem.

Writing in the sand was an old theme when the poet Omar Khayyam wrote "The moving finger writes, and having writ moves on" some four hundred years before Spenser was born. The opening lines of this sonnet evoke both the Bible story of Jesus writing in the sand when a woman caught in adultery was brought

Sir Edmund Spenser

for him to judge and the story of King Canute, who stood at the water's edge and asked his counselors if he could order the tide not to rise.

Commentary

Spenser used archaic spelling here, trying to make his poetry appear antique and respectable. He chose phrasings that were old-fashioned in Chaucer's day. But he is regarded as an innovator for coining many new words and playing with the foreign origins of many English words. In this technique he was joined by many educated writers during the reign of Elizabeth I: Together they enriched the plain, everyday language with words borrowed from Latin and Greek classical writings and from other current dialects of English besides the version that was spoken in and around London.

FACTS

Poetic Imperialism

Critic Harold Bloom wrote:

> Spenser conceived of his poetic function as being a uniquely national one; he wished to write an English poem that would match if not surpass the classical epic of Homer and of Vergil and the contemporary romance of Ariosto and of Tasso. The thrust toward national identity and international greatness that typified Elizabethan aspiration at its most intense is a vital component in Spenser's conscious poetic purpose.[1]

Composing poetry for publication was intended as a political act of nationalism in an international forum. It was a kind of cultural imperialism, more conscious and overt than the modern marketing of American music and films overseas.

Excerpt from

Epithalamion

. . . *Now ceasse ye damsels your delights fore-past;*
Enough it is, that all the day was youres:
Now day is doen, and night is nighing fast,
Now bring the Bryde into the brydall boures.
Now night is come, now soone her disaray,
And in her bed her lay;
Lay her in lilies and in violets,
And silken courteins over her display,
And odoured sheetes, and Arras coverlets.
Behold how goodly my faire love does ly,
In proud humility!
Like unto Maia, when as Jove her took
In Tempe, lying on the flowry gras,
Twixt sleepe and wake, after she weary was,
With bathing in the Acidalian brooke.
Now it is night, ye damsels may be gon,
And leave my love alone,
And leave likewise your former lay to sing:
The woods no more shall answere, nor your echo ring.

Now welcome, night! thou night so long expected,
That long daies labour doest at last defray,
And all my cares, which cruell Love collected,
Has sumd in one, and cancellèd for aye:
Spread thy broad wing over my love and me,
That no man may us see;

And in thy sable mandle us enwrap,
From feare of perrill and foule horror free.
Let no false treason seeke us to entrap,
Nor any dread disquiet once annoy
The safety of our joy:
But let the night be calme, and quietsome,
Without tempestuous storms or sad afray:
Lyke as when Jove with fayre Alcmena lay,
When he begot the great Tirynthian groome:
Or lyke as when he with thy selfe did lie,
And begot Majesty.
And let the mayds and yong men cease to sing;
Ne let the woods them answer nor theyr ecco ring.
...

arras—tapestry
defray—pay for
mandle—cloak
afray—storm

Critical Response To Spenser

Spenser's contemporaries considered him their prince of poets, as fine in English as Virgil was in Latin. He wrote verses in every genre then used, from pastoral and elegy to epic and epithalamion (on marriage). Milton considered Spenser's works taught more and better than the educational essays of St. Thomas Aquinas, a learned man renowned for consideration of his fellow man. When Spenser's treatise on the reformation of Ireland was finally published in 1633, "it showed even then a shrewd comprehension of the problems facing English government in Ireland," according to a later biographer, "and a capacity for political office as thorough as his literary ability."[2]

Suggested Further Reading

A good place to begin is Spenser's *Amoretti*, a cycle of eighty-nine sonnets celebrating his love for Elizabeth Boyle, who became his second wife. Most romantic poetry at that time expressed desire for an unattainable mistress instead. For the literary work of a woman of that time, look to Mary Sidney Herbert, the sister of Philip Sidney, another honored poet.

WILLIAM SHAKESPEARE

(1564–1616)

O n April 26, 1564, William Shakespeare was baptized in Stratford-upon-Avon, the son of John Shakespeare, a yeoman (freeborn farmer working his own property) selling farm produce and hides, and Mary Arden, from a family of aristocrats. The birth date of William Shakespeare is considered to be April 23; infant mortality was high at the time, partly because of the plague, and families commonly waited three days before taking on the expense of baptizing newborns.

Young William was educated first in manners and catechism at a school for young boys, then at a grammar school from age seven to fourteen, where he learned Latin and the classical writings of Greece and Rome. Unable to afford further education, he worked to help support the family, possibly with his father or as a tutor or in other trades.

William Shakespeare

In 1582, Shakespeare married Anne Hathaway. By 1592, Shakespeare had moved to London, working as an actor and playwright with the company the Lord Chamberlain's Men (later the King's Men) performing at court and for the public, supporting his wife and children in Stratford. When the theaters were closed in 1592–1594 because of the plague, his poems *Venus and Adonis* and *The Rape of Lucrece* were published, dedicated to Shakespeare's patron, Henry Wriothesley, Third Earl of Southampton.

Shakespeare is known to have acted in several of his own plays; in *Hamlet*, he played the ghost. His sister's son William Hart played Falstaff. As he became moderately wealthy through writing many plays in blank verse (unrhymed lines of iambic pentameter), Shakespeare reinvested as a part owner of two early theaters, the Globe and Blackfriars. Until 1598 he wrote mainly historical plays and comedies; after about 1601 he wrote his great tragedies and romantic comedies. Some pirated versions of his plays were distributed, and in 1623 his plays were posthumously collected by two members of his company into the First Folio. Shakespeare also wrote a series of 154 sonnets published in 1609, and maintained friendships with many actors and writers.

In 1610, Shakespeare retired to Stratford, where his family still lived and he had maintained business connections. He continued to write. A month after making a will leaving his second-best bed to his wife, Shakespeare died, on April 23, 1616. Buried under the chancel in Holy Trinity Church, Stratford-upon-Avon, his tomb is marked with a stone inscribed:

> Good frend for Jesus sake forbeare,
> To digg the dust encloased heare.
> Bleste be the man who spares thes stones,
> And curst be he that moves my bones.

Sonnet 29

When, in disgrace with Fortune and men's eyes,
I all alone beweep my outcast state,
And trouble deaf heaven with my bootless cries,
And look upon myself, and curse my fate,
Wishing me like to one more rich in hope,
Featured like him, like him with friends possesst,
Desiring this man's art and that man's scope,
With what I most enjoy contented least;
Yet in these thoughts myself almost despising—
Haply I think on thee: and then my state,
Like to the lark at break of day arising
From sullen earth, sings hymns at heaven's gate;
    For thy sweet love rememb'red such wealth brings
    That then I scorn to change my state with Kings.

bootless—useless
haply—fortunately

Summary and Explication

The poet is describing how he feels when outcast from public favor. He cries uselessly and would rather be like someone with better prospects, good looks, and friends. He covets other men's talents and is not content with his usual pleasures. He almost hates himself. But by good luck he remembers his beloved, and his mood rises like a singing bird. Remembering love makes him rich at heart, so he would not trade places with a king.

Poetic Techniques

Shakespeare's version of the sonnet form has a different rhyme scheme from Spenser or the Italian Petrarch. His iambic pentameter lines are rhymed *abab cdcd efef gg*, and the final couplet focuses the reader's attention on the poem's central meaning. Most of the phrases end at the end of a line, except for the moment that changes everything—when he describes remembering love. The *Norton Anthology* notes that the first eight lines "contain a catalogue and the last six turn in quite a different direction."[1]

Themes

Despair, envy, and self-hatred are feelings understood by anyone with ambition and modest income. The restorative qualities of love, though, are desired by anyone. Larks are birds that nest on the ground and fly up into the sky at daybreak or when startled. Shakespeare, inspired by their movement and beautiful song while they rise and descend, is using the lark as a simile for the soul.

Commentary

Like other working writers, Shakespeare wrestled with envy for someone else's abilities, luck, or success. He does not puff himself up with grandeur in this poem that details his sins of despair and envy. And he realizes it is when he leaves introspection behind that he is enriched by love. This sonnet, like many from the collection, has inspired many other poetic works and at least one play.

When Daisies Pied

(from *Love's Labour's Lost*)

Spring

When daisies pied and violets blue
    And lady-smocks all silver-white
And cuckoo-buds of yellow hue
    Do paint the meadows with delight,
The cuckoo then, on every tree,
Mocks married men; for thus sings he,
      Cuckoo!
Cuckoo, cuckoo!—O word of fear,
Unpleasing to a married ear!

When shepherds pipe on oaten straws,
    And merry larks are plowmen's clocks
When turtles tread, and rooks, and daws,
    And maidens bleach their summer smocks,
The cuckoo then, on every tree,
Mocks married men; for thus sings he,
      Cuckoo!
Cuckoo, cuckoo—O word of fear,
Unpleasing to a married ear!

Winter

When icicles hang by the wall
And Dick the shepherd blows his nail,
And Tom bears logs into the hall,
    And milk comes frozen home in pail;
When blood is nipt, and ways be foul,
Then nightly sings the staring owl
      Tu-who!

Tu-whit, Tu-whoo! A merry note!
While greasy Joan doth keel the pot.

When all aloud the wind doth blow,
*   And coughing drowns the parson's saw,*
And birds sit brooding in the snow,
*   And Marian's nose looks red and raw;*
When roasted crabs hiss in the bowl—
Then nightly sings the staring owl
*   Tu-who!*
Tu-whit, Tu-whoo! A merry note!
While greasy Joan doth keel the pot.

cuckoo—cuckoos were a symbol used to mock men whose wives were unfaithful,
    because cuckoo birds lay their eggs in other bird's nests

blows his nail—blows on his fingers to warm them

keel—stir

saw—a wise saying

crabs—crab apples

Dirge

(from *Cymbeline*)

Fear no more the heat o' the sun,
  Nor the furious winter's rages;
Thou thy worldly task hast done,
  Home art gone, and ta'en thy wages:
Golden lads and girls all must,
As chimney-sweepers, come to dust.

Fear no more the frown o' the great;
  Thou art past the tyrant's stroke;
Care no more to clothe and eat;
  To thee the reed is as the oak:
The sceptre, learning, physic, must
All follow this, and come to dust.

Fear no more the lightning-flash,
  Nor the all-dreaded thunder-stone;
Fear not slander, censure rash;
  Thou hast finish'd joy and moan:
All lovers young, all lovers must
Consign to thee, and come to dust.

No exorciser harm thee!
Nor no witchcraft charm thee!
Ghost unlaid forbear thee!
Nothing ill come near thee!
Quiet consummation have;
And renowned be thy grave!

physic—medicine

thunder-stone—a meteorite, or a stone falling from the sky,
 imagined to fall because of thunder and lightning storms

Critical Response To Shakespeare

Shakespeare was not universally admired in his lifetime, but he was praised and earned a steady income. He has come to be regarded by most scholars as the finest English writer without peer, whose talents for poetry and drama are head and shoulders above any other before or since. His dramatic verse is not considered flawlessly perfect but rather the product of sustained effort to interest his audiences, from those who paid a penny for room to stand ankle deep in hazelnut shells, to Queen Elizabeth I (and later her successor, King James I) at court. While many of his plays were written in haste and during rehearsals, his sonnets and other poetry were carefully and deliberated crafted. "The plays contain some of the finest songs ever written," according to the *Norton Anthology of English Literature*. "They illustrate many sides of Shakespeare's genius—his incomparable lyric gift, his ready humor, and his marvellous sensitivity to the sights and sounds

FACTS

Who Wrote Shakespeare?

Some believe the William Shakespeare who wrote poetry was not the author of some or any of the plays credited with his name. There are several contradictory theories. One theory suggests that Shakespeare's name as producer was casually imposed onto plays performed by the company he supported. Another theory suggests that either all his plays or all his poems were written by a nobleman, possibly his patron, who hid his own identity from the taint of public performance. It is, however, quite plausible for one man, largely self-educated after age fourteen, to have written everything credited to Shakespeare.

A poster for *Romeo and Juliet*, one of Shakespeare's most popular plays

of English life, especially the life of the country."[2] His work has never stopped influencing dramatists and poets, and performance of his plays has undergone a revival in many cities across North America.

Suggested Further Reading

Shakespeare himself regarded Christopher Marlowe as a finer writer. Ben Jonson was a friend, rival, and critic of Shakespeare. Though few women were educated at this time, the poetry of Queen Elizabeth I is well worth attention.

JOHN DONNE

(1572–1631)

John Donne was born in 1572, the son of Elizabeth and John Donne, an ironmonger who died while his son was a child. Young John was educated by an uncle who was a priest in the Catholic order of Jesuits. At age eleven, he went to Hart Hall in Oxford, studying for three years, and then to Cambridge for another three years. As a Catholic, he was unable to receive a degree from either university.

Donne then studied law at Lincoln's Inn in London. His faith was badly shaken when his brother died in prison, convicted of sheltering a Catholic priest, which was a criminal offense, as the Protestant government was suppressing Catholicism. This crisis affected his first book, *Satires*, and a collection of love poems called *Songs and Sonnets*. Donne's inheritance allowed him to enjoy wine, women, and song, and he lived recklessly for a time, joining the earl of Essex and Sir Walter Raleigh in an English raid on Cadiz, Spain, in 1596, and an expedition to the Azores. Most of his secular poems were probably written before he was twenty-five.

He ruined his modest but promising civil service career by a secret marriage to his supervisor's young niece, Anne More, in 1601. Her father, who had been trying to arrange a marriage for her with a wealthy nobleman as a business alliance, had Donne dismissed from his post and thrown into Fleet Prison for several weeks. Even so, the marriage was a happy one helped by friends, in spite of a decade of financial worries. Donne worked as a lawyer and wrote his collection of *Divine Poems*, and eventually in 1609 Anne's father gave them her dowry.

Donne wrote articles breaking with his Catholic faith, and he took holy orders as an Anglican minister at King James's insistence that the only post he would ever get would be in the church. He became a popular preacher. For his patron Sir Robert Drury, he wrote *A Funerall Elegie,* on the death of Sir Robert's daughter in 1610, and two anniversary elegies.

Donne was deeply affected when his wife, Anne, died in 1617 while giving birth to their twelfth child, seven of whom survived her. Though in mourning, Donne was able to write his *Holy Sonnets,* dedicated to his patron Magdalen Newport Herbert (mother of George Herbert). He was appointed Dean of St. Paul's Cathedral in London in 1621 and held the post until his death.

While convalescing from a serious illness, Donne wrote *Devotions upon Emergent Occasions,* published in 1624. The most famous of these essays includes the line "No man is an island." Aware that his life was soon to end, Donne preached what came to be called his own funeral sermon, a month before his death on March 31, 1631. Donne's memorial marble effigy survived the Great Fire in 1666 that destroyed the old cathedral and can be seen today in the new St. Paul's. Ten volumes of his sermons have been published.

Engraved by G. Stodart.

John Donne

The Flea

Mark but this flea, and mark in this,
How little that which thou denyst me is;
It sucked me first, and now sucks thee,
And in this flea our two bloods mingled be;
Thou know'st that this cannot be said
A sin, nor shame, nor loss of maidenhead;
  Yet this enjoys before it woo,
  And pampered swells with one blood made of two;
  And this, alas, is more than we would do.

O stay, three lives in one flea spare,
Where we almost, yea, more than married are.
This flea is you and I, and this
Our marriage bed, and marriage temple is.
Though parents grudge, and you, w'are met,
And cloistered in these living walls of jet.
  Though use make you apt to kill me,
  Let not to that self-murder added be,
  And sacrilege, three sins in killing three.

Cruel and sudden, hast thou since
Purpled thy nail in blood of innocence?
Wherein could this flea guilty be,
Except in that drop which it sucked from thee?
Yet thou triumph'st, and say'st that thou
Find'st not thyself nor me the weaker now
  'Tis true; then learn how false fears be:
  Just so much honor, when thou yield'st to me,
  Will waste, as this flea's death took life from thee:

maidenhead—virginity

Summary and Explication

The poet addresses his beloved, saying that what she is denying him is small. The
flea that just bit him has now bit her, and their blood is mingled in it. That is not
a crime. Mixing their blood is like being married. In spite of her parents'
objections, and hers, they are closed up in this black flea. If she kills the flea, his
blood and hers and the sanctity of marriage will all be destroyed. And when she
kills it, it was guilty only of taking one drop of blood. She says that neither she
nor he was weakened by its death. And he says when she yields to him, she will
not lose any more respect than she lost life when the flea died.

Poetic Techniques

These verses of nine lines each alternate between lines in iambic tetrameter and
lines in iambic pentameter, ending with two pentameter lines at the end of each
stanza. The effect leaves the listener expecting more at the end of the short lines
and anticipating what comes next. The verses are also made of rhyming couplets,
with the final line rhyming with the final couplet, in an *aabbccddd* pattern.

Themes

The first theme is of the beloved refusing intimacy. Many poems have various
answers to this dilemma. In this poem the answer is the claim that they already
are intimate, without crime. Any further physical intimacy would have no more
guilt than the fleabite they have already shared.

Commentary

This is one of Donne's metaphysical poems, in which he takes two widely
dissimilar ideas and, in an intellectual and witty discussion, shows how they are
arguably really one idea. Samuel Johnson was later to call Donne the founding
master of the metaphysical poets. In his love poems, Donne demonstrated an
aptitude for making elaborate symbols of love and romance from even the most
unlikely images. Women have been wooed and won with finely crafted verses

about their beauty, or about the great lengths to which a hero would go to win their favor, or about how time is fleeting. Donne is making a seductive poem about being bitten by the same flea: something humble rather than grand, ordinary rather than inspiring, and vulgar rather than refined. It is also intimate, as the pair would have to be close or touching for the flea to leap from him to her. Brian Phillips says in an online study guide:

> This poem is the cleverest of a long line of sixteenth-century love poems using the flea as an erotic image, a genre derived from an older poem of Ovid. Donne's poise of hinting at the erotic without ever explicitly referring to sex, while at the same time leaving no doubt as to exactly what he means, is as much a source of the poem's humor as the silly image of the flea…. [It] gets the point across with a neat conciseness and clarity that Donne's later religious lyrics never attained.[1]

Written as a dramatic monologue, in this poem the poet addresses his beloved in a very direct manner, describing their interaction in clear terms as well as with metaphors and imagery. A dramatic monologue gives the reader a sense of immediacy and of being spoken to directly. Donne made use of this technique often in his poetry, which was circulated widely by hand among his friends but largely went unpublished till after his death.

FACTS

Donne's *Anniversaries*

Ben Jonson told Donne that his *Anniversaries* were blasphemous and profane. If he had been writing about the Virgin Mary, there might have been reasons for this idolatry, Jonson said. But these elegies were written in memory of his patron's fifteen-year-old daughter, Elizabeth Drury, a girl Donne had never even met. This baffled Jonson and other critics, but Donne's intention was to describe the idea of a woman and the progress of a soul.

Holy Sonnet X

Death, be not proud, though some have call'd thee
Mighty and dreadful, for thou art not so:
For those whom thou think'st thou dost overthrow
Die not, poor Death; nor yet canst thou kill me.
From Rest and Sleep, which but thy picture be,
Much pleasure, then from thee much more must flow;
And soonest our best men with thee do go—
Rest of their bones and souls' delivery!
Thou'rt slave to fate, chance, kings, and desperate men,
And dost with poison, war, and sickness dwell;
And poppy or charms can make us sleep as well
And better than thy stroke. Why swell'st thou then?
One short sleep past, we wake eternally,
And Death shall be no more: Death, thou shalt die!

Song

Goe and catche a falling star,
      Get with child a mandrake root,
Tell me where all past years are,
      Or who cleft the Devel's foot;
Teach me to heare mermaids singing,
Or to keep off envy's stinging,
          And find
          What wind
Serves to advance an honest mind.

If thou be'st borne to strange sights,
      Things invisible to see,
Ride ten thousand daies and nights
      Till Age snow white hairs on thee;
Thou, when thou return'st, wilt tell mee
All strange wonders that befell thee,
          And swear
          No where
Lives a woman true and fair.

If thou find'st one, let me know;
      Such a pilgrimage were sweet.
Yet do not; I would not go,
      Though at next door we might meet.
Though she were true when you met her,
And last till you write your letter,
          Yet she
          Will be
False, ere I come, to two or three.

Critical Response To Donne

It is too easy to consider Donne as a poet who divided his talents between devotional verse and libertine songs. The same acute perceptions and precise wit is found in both his secular writing and his *Holy Sonnets*. It is rare to find a poet who can write of the mind in its many capacities, and, as Harold Bloom says, "Eloquence and shrewdness in behalf of the invisible are not often so combined."[2]

The quickness and acuteness of Donne's poetic wit gave ambivalent and uneasy feelings, first to Ben Jonson, then to his fellow neoclassical poets Alexander Pope and Samuel Johnson. To them, Donne seemed to take metaphor too far. After the neoclassical poets, the romantic poets took great interest in Donne's works. Oddly enough, he was later considered an "anti-romantic" by T. S. Eliot, who also admired the poetry of Donne.

Suggested Further Reading

The best place to start reading Donne's works is with *Songs and Sonnets*, and after that his *Holy Sonnets*. Though Donne had an uncanny respect for women's minds, and it can be argued that his works show it, the works of Amelia Lanier show by the incidents she describes that this respect was not common at that time.

George Herbert

(1593–1633)

On April 3, 1593, George Herbert was born to an eminent Welsh family in Montgomery, Wales. His father, Richard Herbert, died in 1596, leaving ten children for his mother, Magdalen Newport Herbert, to raise and educate. She was a great literary patron of distinguished writers. In gratitude, John Donne dedicated his *Holy Sonnets* to her.

At age ten, young George went to Westminster School and won a scholarship to Trinity College in Cambridge. He earned his bachelor's degree in arts in 1613 and his master's degree in 1616 and was elected a major fellow of Trinity. He was appointed reader in Rhetoric at Cambridge two years later, and then in 1620 he was elected public orator, a post he kept with pleasure for seven years. His duties included representing Cambridge at public occasions with dignified and florid Latin statements.

George Herbert

Elected as a Member of Parliament for Montgomery in 1624 and 1625, Herbert enjoyed the favor of King James I. He contributed a memorial poem in Latin when Sir Francis Bacon died, a year after dedicating his own *Translation of Certaine Psalmes* to Herbert. But with the death of the king in 1625, and later the deaths of two influential patrons and his mother, Herbert gave up his secular political career. He married Jane Danvers in 1629 and took holy orders in the Church of England in 1630. The last years of his life were spent as rector in Bremerton, a rural parish near Salisbury and London.

There Herbert rebuilt the church with his own funds, preached, and wrote poetry. He earned the respect of his parishioners, who called him "Holy Mr. Herbert." His manual of practical advice to country parsons, *A Priest to the Temple*, was published later in 1652. Poor health and tuberculosis (or consumption, as it was then called) caused his death on March 1, 1633.

On his deathbed, Herbert sent a manuscript of poetry to his good friend Nicholas Ferrar, the founder of a religious community, asking him to publish the poems only if he thought they might be helpful to "any dejected poor soul."[1] Published in 1633, this collection of poems became Herbert's major published work, *The Temple: Sacred Poems and Private Ejaculations.*

FACTS

A Private Poet

During his life, Herbert enjoyed his work as an orator and later as rector. But except for a few poems he showed his mother as a young man, and a few he presented on important occasions, such as the death of Sir Francis Bacon, Herbert kept his poetry private. "Like Marvell, Hopkins, and Emily Dickinson," says Harold Bloom, "Herbert avoided publication in his own lifetime."[2] It is likely that most of his poems were written during his time as rector in Bremerton.

Jordan

Who sayes that fictions onely and false hair
Become a verse? Is there in truth no beautie?
Is all good structure in a winding stair?
May no lines passe, except they do their dutie
    Not to a true, but painted chair?

Is it no verse, except enchanted groves
And sudden arbours shadow coarse-spunne lines?
Must purling streams refresh a lover's loves?
Must all be vail'd, while he that reades, divines,
    Catching the sense at two removes?

Shepherds are honest people; let them sing:
Riddle who list, for me, and pull for Prime:
I envie no mans nightingale or spring;
Nor let them punish me with losse of ryme,
    Who plainly say, My God, My King.

list—pull in a direction, as a ship lists in the wind or a harnessed horse
    resists its reins

pull for prime—draw the lucky card in the parlor game primeo; also,
    go your own way

Summary and Explication

Herbert is writing here of his opinion regarding popular poetry. He asks if poems can tell only made-up stories in fancy-dress wigs. Isn't there beauty in the truth? Plain buildings are good, not only fancy spiral staircases. Is poetry accepted only when it praises artistic images instead of real objects? Is it poetry just because magical forests are described, even though the words are clumsy? Can love be described only in certain ways? He asks if the reader always has to guess the meaning of a metaphor about a metaphor about reality. Shepherds can sing their own songs. Tell riddles if you want, for all he cares, and do your own thing. He does not covet the beauty other people see, and he will not let anyone say he is not writing a poem when he uses plain words to talk about God.

Poetic Techniques

This poem is written in rhyming verses of five lines each, and the lines are in iambic pentameter. The stresses are not consistently iambic, but that is common in blank verse as well as in these rhymed lines. The last line of each of these three verses has only four stressed syllables, not five. This technique makes the reader pause at these short lines. It adds particular emphasis and draws the reader's attention. The technique can also be seen in the Anglo-Saxon poem "Wulf and Eadwacer" and in Keats's poem "This Living Hand."

The last syllable of each line rhymes with other lines in the rhyme scheme *ababa, cdcdc, efefe*. The first line, *a*, rhymes with the third and fifth lines. Though not a fourteen-line sonnet, this poem is clearly influenced by the sonnet form. The effect of an additional line on a reader or listener familiar with sonnets is subtle and firm, even on modern readers who may not realize how many sonnets they have read or heard as songs or hymns. It makes this poem's final, fifteenth, line more noticed, and it confirms the importance of the statement that ends a poem filled with questions.

Herbert opens with a question, asking who says there is only one way to write poetry, and he ends with the statement that he will not let anyone say his plain words are not poetry. And he does use plain words in this poem, choosing phrases that are easy to say aloud, and no uncommon words except when he asks if those fancy phrases really must be used.

Themes

Herbert is celebrated, along with John Donne, as one of the metaphysical poets, because much of his poetry celebrates his love for God. Love also figures earlier in the poem, in the eighth line. In the sixteenth and early seventeenth centuries, there was a popular fashion among the English and French nobility to idealize the lives of shepherds raising their flocks of pretty lambs, with plenty of time for romantic love. Many pastoral poems, plays, and operas were written by men who had never done a hard day's farm labor in their lives. Christopher Marlowe and many others wrote romantic verse about shepherds and shepherdesses finding true love while wandering through fields of spring flowers. When attending special dances and games, aristocratic women and men wore elaborate wigs and brocaded and embroidered costumes supposed to be like those of shepherds.

As a rector in a rural parish, Herbert was familiar with the farming community he served. In this poem, Herbert states his opinion very clearly: Shepherds can sing their own songs. Poetry can describe plain reality. "Pull for prime" he says, referring both to looking out for Number One and also to drawing a lucky card in the parlor game of primeo. Poetry does not need to be made fancy and artificially pretty nor dressed up in silly detailed metaphors.

Commentary

Samuel Johnson wrote in his essays a series of strictures against religious poetry a century after Herbert's death, declaring that though the essence of poetry is invention, producing unexpected surprises and delights, the topics of devotion are few and universally known. That was no barrier for Herbert, whose verses spoke to many of his readers about their own perceptions. "Shepherds are honest people; let them sing," he said. He believed that educated poets should not pretend that their inventive talent produces the only worthwhile poems. It is also poetry when ordinary folk make verses about their own lives, even and perhaps especially when describing perceptions that are universally known.

Modern poets, the Canadian poet Milton Acorn most of all, owe much to George Herbert's plain verse and this poem in particular. He prefers to speak in plain words, and that gives honesty and impact to the final words of this poem.

Sir Walter Raleigh and many others wrote replies to Marlowe's poem "The Passionate Shepherd to His Love" (which begins, "Come live with me and be my love/And we will all the pleasures prove"). "Jordan" is Herbert's reply.

Love

Love bade me welcome; yet my soul drew back,
Guilty of dust and sin.
But quick-eyed Love, observing me grow slack
From my first entrance in,
Drew nearer to me, sweetly questioning
If I lacked anything.

'A guest,' I answer'd, 'worthy to be here':
Love said, 'You shall be he.'
'I, the unkind, ungrateful? Ah, my dear,
I cannot look on thee.'
Love took my hand, and smiling did reply,
'Who made the eyes but I?'

'Truth, Lord; but I have marr'd them; let my shame
Go where it doth deserve.'
'And know you not,' says Love, 'Who bore the blame?'
'My dear, then I will serve.'
'You must sit down,' says Love, 'and taste my meat.'
So I did sit and eat.

The Church-floore

Mark you the floore? that square and speckled stone,
　　Which looks so firm and strong,
　　　　Is Patience:

And th' other black and grave, wherewith each one
　　Is checker'd all along,
　　　　Humilitie:

The gentle rising, which on either hand
　　Leads to the Quire above,
　　　　Is Confidence:

But the sweet cement, which in one sure band
　　Ties the whole frame, is Love
　　　　And Charitie.

Hither sometimes Sinne steals, and stains
The marbles neat and curious veins:
But all is cleansed when the marble weeps.
Sometimes Death, puffing at the doore,
Blows all the dust about the floore:
But while he thinks to spoil the room, he sweeps.
Blest be the Architect, whose art
Could build so strong in a weak heart.

quire—a raised alcove or balcony where the church choir
　gathers to sing

Critical Response To Herbert

The poems collected in *The Temple* discuss the architectural style of churches and the rebuilding of Bremerton church, in psychological and metaphysical terms as well as in visual layout and the meaning of the words. On publication, these poems were astonishingly well received, not only by friends and family but also by readers and critics at large. Over the next fifty years there were at least thirteen printings of this popular and acclaimed work. Later, Samuel Coleridge was to praise Herbert's poetic diction as pure, manly, and unaffected.

His direct approach and clear imagery were of great interest to many readers. Looking through his other poems, it is clear that Herbert was also capable of seeking out "quaint words, and trim invention … curling with metaphors a plain intention."[3] He seems to have been more familiar with John Donne's erotic poetry than with Donne's *Holy Sonnets*, complaining in *The Temple* that poetry seemed only to serve erotic love.

Suggested Further Reading

As one of the metaphysical poets, Herbert has been overshadowed by the more famous John Donne, but Donne wrote poetry on other matters as well. For a woman's voice of that time, look to Anne Bradstreet. Readers wanting to know more about George Herbert from a contemporary perspective can seek out an old book by Izaak Walton (1593–1683), *The Lives of John Donne and George Herbert.*

JOHN MILTON
(1608–1674)

John Milton was born in Cheapside, London, on December 9, 1608. His father, John Milton, was a prosperous scrivener, a legal secretary who prepared and notarized documents as well as conducting real estate transactions and money lending, and he was also a composer of church music and madrigals who had become Protestant. His deeply religious mother, Sarah Jeffrey, was the daughter of a merchant sailor.

Young John was educated by his father and then at St. Paul's School and Christ's College in Cambridge, where his classmates called him "the Lady," making fun of his long hair and attention to his appearance. While in school he wrote poetry in Latin, Italian, and English. Preparing for a career in the church or politics, he studied and read much more than his schoolwork. From childhood, his poor eyesight was further harmed by study, and he also suffered from headaches.

After graduating cum laude (with honors), Milton returned to his father's house and did not take up a trade but instead wrote poetry. His works at that time included *L'Allegro, Il Penseroso*, the masque or musical performance *Comus*, and *Lycidas* (an elegy written after his friend Edward King died). From Chaucer's lifetime to Milton's time, the Italian Renaissance was admired and the poetic works of Dante were revered to such an extent that Englishmen often named the titles and characters of their poems and plays in Latin or Italian and freely borrowed settings and plots from Italy. Like many prosperous young men, Milton toured the continent. He met with intellectuals and Galileo, now aging and blind and under house arrest. Milton also began planning to write a series of tragedies and epics. Returning to London in 1639, he started a small school for his nephews and a few other pupils.

Three times, Milton married much younger women. His first marriage was in 1642 to Mary Powell, who was only seventeen and who returned to her parents' home for three years soon after the wedding. In spite of her family being Royalists in the Civil War, Milton reconciled with Mary when she returned to his home, bringing her parents with her. They had three daughters together—Anne, Mary, and Deborah, who outlived both their parents.

In 1641, Milton began writing what became over twenty years a series of controversial pamphlets written from a Puritan Protestant viewpoint defending religious and civil rights, campaigning against the authority of the bishops and in favor of democracy. His tracts advocating divorce for incompatibility were a scandal in Parliament and to the Royalists and the Anglican clergy. Attempts to censor these works led Milton to defend freedom of the press in another tract.

After the public execution of King Charles I in 1649, Oliver Cromwell's government appointed Milton Secretary of Foreign Tongues. He wrote articles defending the new government and responding to statements from foreign nations. His physician warned him that study was ruining the last of his vision, which had been suffering for some ten years, but Milton persisted in writing.

These articles had considerable lasting influence upon his fellow Puritans and later the men at the forefront of the American Revolution.

The year 1652 brought many losses for Milton. In February he lost his sight. In May, Mary gave birth to their third daughter, Deborah, and died a few days later. In June, their one-year-old son John died. Milton married Katherine Woodcock in 1656, but she and their only child, an infant daughter, died in 1658. He dedicated his sonnet "On His Deceased Wife" to her memory.

After Cromwell's death in 1658 and the publication of two tracts, or pamphlets, defending republican government in early 1659, Milton went into hiding. Two of his earlier tracts defending the Commonwealth were publicly burned that June in Paris and Toulouse, France. Milton was arrested as a propagandist and defender of the Commonwealth, but Andrew Marvell and other men of influence spoke out for him in Parliament. He paid a massive fine and was released before Christmas. The English monarchy was restored under Charles II in 1660. Milton escaped further punishment despite threats from radical Royalists.

The English Civil War

Protestants and Catholics jostled for primacy in the politics and society of England, but during Milton's lifetime the conflict came to a peak with the Civil War. Many, but not all, Protestants supported Cromwell's Commonwealth. Among the Protestants, the Puritans pressed for simpler ceremonies of faith and worship than those established by law for the Church of England, and they regarded luxury and pleasure as sinful. The majority of the emigrants who settled in New England were Puritans.

John Milton

He married his third wife, Elizabeth Minshull, in 1663 when she was twenty-four, and though his daughters had opposed the match, he lived happily with Elizabeth. In his later years he was kept very busy tutoring students and dictating his epic poems. In November 1674, he died peacefully of gout. There is a monument to Milton in Poets' Corner in Westminster Abbey, but he was buried next to his father in the church of St. Giles, Cripplegate.

An Epitaph on the Admirable Dramatic Poet W. Shakespeare

What needs my Shakespeare for his honour'd Bones
The labour of an age in piled stones,
Or that his hallow'd reliques should be hid
Under a Star-y pointing Pyramid?
Dear son of memory, great heir of fame,
What need'st thou such weak witnes of thy name?
Thou in our wonder and astonishment
Hast built thyself a live-long Monument.
For whilst to th' shame of slow-endeavouring art
Thy easie numbers flow, and that each heart
Hath from the Leaves of thy unvalu'd book
Those Delphick lines with deep impression took,
Then thou our fancy of it self bereaving,
Dost make us marble with too much conceaving;
And so sepulchr'd in such pomp dost lie,
That Kings for such a Tomb would wish to die.

Summary and Explication

Milton is describing his respect for Shakespeare's writing. Shakespeare does not need a pyramid to be remembered. He has built a wonderful monument of words that read naturally, unlike some writers' painfully complicated writing, and everyone who reads Shakespeare's priceless words has been impressed by his mysterious wisdom. We stand still, thinking about his writing. Even kings want to be remembered with such respect.

Poetic Techniques

These rhyming couplets are written in iambic pentameter. Milton is consciously reaching for a grand tone, with references to ancient Egypt and Greece, and all the ceremony with which great kings were buried. The thirteenth and fourteenth lines have two-syllable rhymes (called female rhymes, as one-syllable rhymes are called male); female rhyme is almost always a sign of humor in English poetry, and right on cue the fourteenth line cracks a joke, saying that thinking of Shakespeare's words will turn people into stone. The structure of his lines is both archaic and contrived, and because this is almost too much, the poem is brought to an end quickly, with a reference to Shakespeare's own twenty-ninth sonnet.

Themes

The tombs of kings are intended as lasting monuments, not only to the king as a person and leader, but also to the king's people and culture. The Great Pyramid of Cheops, or Khufu, is suggested by the poem's first four lines. Milton states that Shakespeare's writing was a similarly impressive work, which built up wonder in each reader instead of piling stones. By calling his lines "Delphic," Milton suggests that they are mysteriously inspired by unseen spiritual powers of the Creation and the Underworld, like the words uttered by the Oracle or Prophetess at Delphi.

And when people are still, perhaps reading the Second Folio or watching a play being performed, Milton says they become marble. This is a reference to the marble statues gracing the tombs of Renaissance kings and popes. But Shakespeare is honored in a better way, by his audience's respect.

Commentary

During his tour of the continent, Milton visited Italy. He would have seen fine marble statues in Florence and Rome, and possibly the matchless papal tomb that Michelangelo carved, adorned with marble figures. The great men of English culture were still disappointed that England had nothing so fine as the art and science of the Italian Renaissance, when this, Milton's first published poem, appeared anonymously in the Second Folio of Shakespeare's writing in 1632.

He wrote in what can be called "the grand style" rather than a relaxed and natural style, a manner of grandeur rather than of grandiosity. This did not serve well in his efforts at humor. He was by no means a modern writer nor even a typical writer of the English Renaissance. His influences were biblical, classical, and, to a lesser extent, medieval.

Excerpt from
Paradise Lost

. . . what in me is dark
Illumine, what is low raise and support,
That to the heighth of this great argument,
I may assert Eternal Providence,
And justify the ways of God to men.

Summary and Explication

Milton is invoking the Muse, asking for inspiration that will bring him
understanding, like light to the blind or a crutch to one who is bent and fallen.
He wants his poetry to defend God as the eternal provider, as if he were
defending God's treatment of men in Parliament or a court of law or defending
God's decisions before an assembly of men. Milton does mean "men" here; he
could have ended the line with "all." That God's treatment of women is not being
justified, or justified to women, is a foreshadowing of an event later in poem: the
first sin, which occurred when Eve gave in to the temptation to eat the forbidden
fruit of the tree of knowledge of Good and Evil.

Sonnet XXIII
On His Deceased Wife

Methought I saw my late espousèd Saint
Brought to me like Alcestis from the grave,
Whom Jove's great son to her glad Husband gave,
Rescu'd from death by force though pale and faint.
Mine as whom washt from spot of child-bed taint
Purification in the old Law did save,
And such, as yet once more I trust to have
Full sight of her in Heaven without restraint,
Came vested all in white, pure as her mind:
Her face was vail'd; yet to my fancied sight,
Love, sweetness, goodness, in her person shin'd
So clear, as in no face with more delight.
But O as to embrace me she enclin'd,
I wak'd, she fled, and day brought back my night.

Summary and Explication

"My late espousèd Saint" is Milton's wife Elizabeth, who had recently died and so was believed to be among the saints and angels in Heaven. Milton felt, since Elizabeth had died because of bearing his child, that she was like Alcestis, a queen from Greek history. When Admetus was condemned by the gods to die, he allowed his wife Alcestis to give up her life in his place, but he felt guilt and misery for doing so. Alcestis was brought back from Hades by Heracles. Milton dreamed he saw his late wife Elizabeth, dressed in pure white as a saint because she had died in a state of grace. She would have been veiled during a blessing called "The Churching of Women"—a ceremony of purification and thanksgiving for survival of childbirth. In his dream, Milton could see her face, but as she came to embrace him, he woke and remembered that he was blind and that she was dead.

Milton's Blindness

The cause of Milton's blindness may have been glaucoma, made worse by overuse of his eyes. But even blindness did not limit his descriptive powers and poetic imagery. With the help of many assistants such as Andrew Marvell, Milton not only continued to write more articles, but in his later years he also created the greatest of his poetry. He composed verse after long verse in his head at night, and in the morning he recited the lines to his daughter Deborah, nephews, friends, and other assistants for transcription.

In this engraving, the blind Milton dictates *Paradise Lost* to his daughters.

Critical Response To Milton

Though Milton did not enjoy much financial success from the epic verses he wrote late in life, he received considerable critical praise. Dryden said of *Paradise Lost*: "This man cuts us all out, and the ancients too."[1] He is regarded by most literary scholars as second only to Shakespeare.

Not all critics praise Milton. Many poets of that time thought that nothing new really remained to be done with sonnets, but Milton disagreed. T. S. Eliot described Milton as having his sensuousness "withered by book learning," and claimed that reading his poetry could only be an influence for the worse."[2] But Milton deeply influenced the romantic poets, including Blake and Shelley, who recognized that the protagonist of *Paradise Lost* is the fallen angel Lucifer/Satan.

Paradise Lost inspired and influenced many works of art, including Haydn's oratorio *The Creation, The Rape of the Lock* and *The Dunciad* by Pope, *Endymion* by Keats, *The Vision of Judgement by Lord Byron,* and *The Lord of the Rings* by J.R.R. Tolkien.

Suggested Further Reading

Of Milton's works, perhaps *Paradise Lost* and *Samson Agonistes* are most interesting for a modern reader. For the work of a professional woman writer of that time, look to Aphra Behn or Katherine Phillips.

ALEXANDER POPE
(1688–1744)

Alexander Pope was born May 21, 1688, in London, the son of Edith Turner Pope and Alexander Pope, a linen merchant who had converted to Catholicism. Both their families had divided along Catholic and Protestant lines. Young Alexander's education was frequently interrupted. His aunt taught him to read at home. Twyford School expelled him for writing a satire on one of the teachers. By age twelve he was writing verses and reading books from his father's library. A local priest taught him Latin and Greek, and later he studied French and Italian poetry.

In 1700, the family moved to Binfield, obeying a new act of Parliament prohibiting Catholics from living within ten miles of London. Young Alexander had previously been healthy and had even survived being trampled on by a cow, but in Binfield he caught tuberculosis through infected milk. His spine

A group of images—drawings, printed material, and music—
relating to Alexander Pope

was badly affected, making him only four feet six inches tall even though he wore a stiffened canvas bodice to support his spine. All his life he suffered from headaches and asthma.

After moving to London, Pope published at age twenty-three his first major work, *An Essay on Criticism*, written in rhyming couplets. Pope's work made a good impression on the dramatist William Wycherley, who introduced him into fashionable London literary circles in 1704. His *Pastorals*, published in 1709, brought him public attention. Associating first with friends who were anti-Catholic Whigs, by 1713 he had Tory sympathies and joined the Scriblerus club, a literary group that satirized pretentious erudition. He was able to interest sufficient subscribers in his work to translate first the *Iliad* and then the *Odyssey* from Greek into English, publishing each book as he finished translating it, which made him possibly the first Englishman to earn his living solely as a poet, not a dramatist or playwright, and with no patrons financing his expenses.

He took a long lease on a house and five acres in Twickenham, about fifteen miles from London, and studied horticulture and landscape gardening. In his back garden, which attracted many visiting writers, statesmen, beauties, and the Prince of Wales, he built a romantic "grot" or grotto in a tunnel linked to the Thames River. He died May 30, 1744, at his home.

FACTS

British Politics

The House of Parliament was largely divided into two parties: the Tories and the Whigs. A Tory was likely to be a hereditary landowner who favored stable economics in government and policies supporting high rates of employment among the working class, who by their labor supported landowners. A Whig was likely to be a noble whose wealth was in business rather than land, and who favored policies supporting business owners and profiteers.

Excerpt from

The Rape of the Lock

An Heroi-Comical Poem

Not with more Glories, in th' Etherial Plain,
The Sun first rises o'er the purpled Main,
Than issuing forth, the Rival of his Beams
Lanch'd on the Bosom of the Silver Thames.
Fair Nymphs, and well-drest Youths around her shone,
But ev'ry Eye was fix'd on her alone.
On her white Breast a sparkling Cross she wore,
Which Jews might kiss, and Infidels adore.
Her lively Looks a sprightly Mind disclose,
Quick as her Eyes, and as unfix'd as those:

Favours to none, to all she Smiles extends,
Oft she rejects, but never once offends.
Bright as the Sun, her Eyes the Gazers strike,
And, like the sun, they shine on all alike.
Yet graceful Ease, and Sweetness void of Pride,
Might hide her Faults, if Belles had faults to hide:
If to her share some Female Errors fall,
Look on her Face, and you'll forget 'em all.

This Nymph, to the Destruction of Mankind,
Nouris'd two Locks, which graceful hung behind
In equal Curls, and well conspir'd to deck
With shining Ringlets her smooth Iv'ry Neck.
Love in these Labyrinths his Slaves detains,
And mighty Hearts are held in slender Chains.
With hairy Sprindges we the Birds betray,
Slight Lines of Hair surprize the Finny Prey,
Fair Tresses Man's Imperial Race insnare,
And Beauty draws us with a single Hair.

Th' Adventrous Baron the bright Locks admir'd,
He saw, he wish'd, and to the Prize aspir'd:
Resolv'd to win, he meditates the way,
By Force to ravish, or by Fraud betray;
For when Success a Lover's Toil attends,
Few ask, if Fraud or Force attain'd his Ends.

For this, e're Phoebus rose, he had implor'd
Propitious Heav'n, and ev'ry Pow'r ador'd,
But chiefly Love—to Love an Altar built,
Of twelve vast French Romances, neatly gilt.
There lay three Garters, half a Pair of Gloves;
And all the Trophies of his former Loves.
With tender Billet-doux he lights the Pyre,
And breathes three am'rous Sighs to raise the Fire.
Then prostrate falls, and begs with ardent Eyes
Soon to obtain, and long possess the Prize:
The Pow'rs gave Ear, and granted half his Pray'r,
The rest, the Winds dispers'd in empty Air.

sprindges—bird traps

Phoebus—the sun; Phoebus-Apollo was the Greek god of the sun

billet-doux—love letters

Summary and Explication

The rising sun is no brighter than Belinda, the unnamed young woman who is the center of attention as she goes in a boat upon the Thames River. Other fair young people are there, but everyone is looking at her. Everyone adores her like an idol; even Jews and Muslims, who make no religious icons, would kiss the Christian symbol because it is lying on her breast. Her mind, her expressions, and feelings are active but not fixed on any one thing or person. She is so beautiful, she would be forgiven for any fault. She has two locks of hair curled on her neck. Love can trap us like birds and fishes are caught.

The Baron admires her hair and resolves to have it. Before dawn he prayed at an altar made of his trophies of love that he would soon have his prize and keep it a long time. Half his prayer was granted, but the rest went up in smoke.

Poetic Techniques

These lines of iambic pentameter are rhyming couplets, arranged in long verses grouped into sections or "books" like an epic poem. However, the *Iliad* and the *Aeneid* are not so crammed with flowery adjectives and a long-winded, saccharine malice. The grandiose styling has a thoroughly pompous air, and it teeters toward the ridiculous like a powdered beauty on high-heeled shoes with a towering hairstyle.

Themes

Belinda is described as bright as Phoebus Apollo, the Greek god of the sun and poets. She is not only beautiful, but she also has intelligence; but it is not directed toward any goal, just as her affections are not focused upon any one person. Pope considers this an error, but she is too beautiful to blame for anything.

The Baron's prayer is a very pagan ritual, well suited for satire or ridicule both by a Catholic believing he has the one true faith and by Protestant readers who shunned idolatry in any form.

Commentary

The Rape of the Lock originated in a trivial event in 1711, when young Robert, Lord Petre, cut off a lock of hair from Arabella Fermor, whom he had been courting. A mutual friend suggested that Pope make a humorous poem about this offense, which had caused a schism to develop between their families. The resulting poem became "the finest mock-heroic or mock-epic poem in English … exquisitely witty and balanced burlesque," as David Cody wrote in an online introduction to the poem. "It functions at once … as an implicit indictment of human pride, and a revelation of the essentially trivial nature of many of the aspects of human existence which we tend to hold dear."[1]

Pope was a great admirer of the Roman poets Horace and Vergilius, but he was not writing verses here about heroes and gods, merely ordinary people who took themselves far too seriously. "Know then thyself, presume not God to scan," he wrote later in his *Essay on Man*. "The proper study of Mankind is Man."

FACTS

Editing Shakespeare

Pope prepared a new edition of Shakespeare in 1725, without making note that he had "regularized" the Bard's meter and rewritten his verse in several places. When scholars attacked this edition, Pope took great offense, particularly against Lewis Theobald. Pope's response was his satire *The Dunciad* in 1728, a savage burlesque ridiculing bad writers, scientists, and critics, with Theobald as its primary target. Before he died, Pope expanded and revised *The Dunciad* with a new mock-hero as "king of dunces": the poet laureate Colley Cibber.

You know where you did despise

You know where you did despise
(Tother day) my little Eyes,
Little Legs, and little Thighs,
And some things, of little Size,
You know where.

You, tis true, have fine black eyes,
Taper legs, and tempting Thighs,
Yet what more than all we prize
Is a Thing of little Size,
You know where.

Summary and Explication

When a woman spoke rudely of Pope's disabilities, even guessing publicly that his private parts were small, Pope wrote this reply. Even a little man is valued more than a pretty woman, he says, because he is a man.

The Age of the Enlightenment may have come, but attitudes about disabled people were certainly not generally enlightened, and women were not even legally recognized as persons by the British Privy Council until 1929. Pope was the constant target of vicious comments about his disabilities, comments that would not be tolerated today at public gatherings or in the media. This poem shows that his response was equally vicious; he fought dirty, but without descending to vulgar words.

Solitude: An Ode

How happy he, who free from care
The rage of courts, and noise of towns;
Contented breathes his native air,
     In his own grounds.

Whose herds with milk, whose fields with bread,
Whose flocks supply him with attire,
Whose trees in summer yield him shade,
     In winter fire.

Blest! Who can unconcern'dly find
Hours, days, and years slide swift away,
In health of body, peace of mind,
     Quiet by day,

Sound sleep by night; study and ease
Together mix'd; sweet recreation,
And innocence, which most does please,
     With meditation.

Thus let me live, unheard, unknown;
Thus unlamented let me die;
Steal from the world, and not a stone
     Tell where I lie.

Critical Response To Pope

The Rape of the Lock secured Pope's reputation as a leading poet of his time. He became famous for witty satires and bitter, aggressive quarrels with other writers. Though he accepted assistance from William Broome and Elijah Fenton in translating the *Odyssey*, he did not give credit to his assistants' contributions. "Sure he is fond of being hated," wrote Broome in a letter. "I wonder he is not thrashed: but his littleness is his protection; no man shoots a wren."[2] After preparing an edition of his correspondence, tailored to his own advantage, Pope tried to make it look like the book was released by London's most unscrupulous publisher against his wishes. His hunched back became a constant target for literary critics slinging insults. He had more enemies than any English writer, before or since, and was fiercely loyal to his friends.

The first half of the eighteenth century has always been considered the Age of Pope and of Jonathan Swift. After Pope's death, his reputation declined. The romantic poets, except for Lord Byron, had little time for him. In the Victorian era, Pope was dismissed for artificial diction, too-regular versification, and inhumane satires. It was not until the 1930s that his work began to be respected again.

Suggested Further Reading

The Pastorals and *The Rape of the Lock* would probably be of more interest to younger readers than Pope's other works. Pope supported and encouraged Jonathan Swift in his writing. Anne Finch was another poet of their time, and several of her poems contain references to Pope's works.

10

SAMUEL JOHNSON

(1709–1784)

On September 18, 1709, Samuel Johnson was born in Lichfield in Staffordshire. His father was Michael Johnson, a bookseller and stationer. His mother, Sara, was unable to nurse him, and young Samuel caught scrofula from a wet nurse. This infection, a form of tuberculosis, made him deaf in his left ear, blind in that eye, and with dim vision in the other. His face was also scarred and was further disfigured by smallpox. Throughout his life, he fiercely resisted any temptation to self-indulgence or self-pity because of his disabilities. An uncle who was a local boxing champion taught him to fight, and years later Johnson walked in the worst parts of London without fear of robbers.

He studied in the local grammar school under a headmaster who beat students. When Johnson turned nineteen in 1728, his mother's small inheritance was just enough to enable him to study for a year at Oxford, but he had to leave without completing his degree. He wrote "The Young Author"—a short poem about the almost certain destruction of great dreams.

Two years of depression followed. Johnson worked in his father's bookstall and in a school and developed convulsive twitches and tics that made strangers think he was an idiot. But meeting the Porters, a prosperous merchant family who thought him sensible and good company, restored his confidence. After Henry Porter died, his widow Elizabeth became close friends with Johnson. They were married in 1735, in a love match though she was twenty years older. Johnson opened a boy's school with Elizabeth's dowry of over 600 pounds, but closed it after a year with insufficient pupils.

They went to London, where he worked as a freelance writer and columnist for ten years before taking a commission to write the first English dictionary. Johnson also wrote poetry and a series of 208 moral essays, which he self-published twice a week for two years. Once he wrote a fine essay on idleness and procrastination in great haste while the printer's boy waited to run with it to the press. Sadly, his wife's health failed, and she died in 1752.

FACTS

Johnson's Moral Compass

Johnson continually examined his own mind and actions for any moral error or hypocrisy. He sent his Negro (as people of African descent were called) servant, Francis Barber, to school. His appetite was legendary, and he could drink over twenty-five cups of tea at one sitting, but during years of poverty he often skipped supper in order to tip his dinner waiter a penny. In 1779, he would share his penny breakfasts with Robert Levet, a humble doctor among the poor. Hester Thrale observed that he loved the poor, bringing lame or sick people into his house and giving all his small coins to beggars. For years, when walking home at night, he put pennies into the hands of children asleep in doorways.

Dr. Samuel Johnson

Unlike the committees that took decades to write the Italian and French dictionaries, Johnson worked in one room and took nine years to complete the assignment by 1755, with the help of six copyists who helped him find quotations in borrowed books as examples for the word definitions. Oxford University awarded him a Master of Arts degree for this work.

Almost immediately he took on a commission to prepare a definitive new edition of Shakespeare's works, with notes, analysis, and commentary. The prime minister awarded Johnson a pension for life of 300 pounds a year in 1762. Johnson was persuaded to accept it as a reward for his service to his country in writing the dictionary, and this gave him the financial security he had never known. He continued to write poetry and articles.

The Shakespeare work took nine years, and Dublin University gave him an honorary doctoral degree in 1765. But depression gripped him again. His friends Henry and Hester Thrale took him into their home and helped him recover. In 1775, Oxford gave him an honorary doctorate. Johnson took on a project to write biographies of fifty-two English poets since 1660 and finished it in 1781.

Johnson suffered a stroke in 1783. He recovered to some extent, but his health was failing, and he died on December 13, 1784. He was buried in Westminster Abbey.

Excerpt from
On the Death of Robert Levet

Condemn'd to Hope's delusive mine,
As on we toil from day to day,
By sudden blasts or slow decline,
Our social comforts drop away.

Well tried, through many a varying year,
See Levet to the grave descend,
Officious, innocent, sincere,
Of ev'ry friendless name the friend....

In Misery's darkest cavern known,
His useful care was ever nigh,
Where hopeless Anguish pour'd his groan
And lonely Want retired to die.

No summons mock'd by chill delay,
No petty gain disdain'd by pride;
The modest wants of every day
The toil of every day supplied.

His virtues walk'd their narrow round,
Nor made a pause, nor left a void;
And sure th' Eternal Master found
The single talent well employ'd. . . .

Summary and Explication

The poet is speaking of his friend's worthy life. While hope fools people into working every day, public services disappear slowly or suddenly, as fire can bring a building down or patrons lose interest. After many challenging years, Levet is being buried, friend to the friendless. He helped miserable people, always came when called, and was glad to make small improvements. Daily needs were met by daily work. He did his duty; he had one skill and put it to good use.

Poetic Techniques

These short four-line verses are written in iambic tetrameter, making this poem an odd combination of a tribute written in the grand manner and a plain spoken-word eulogy. Iambic pentameter was commonly used for blank verse and writing on grand matters, while four-line verses in tetrameter were more commonly seen in anonymous folk songs and ballads. The four-beat lines and grim, brave tone are an echo of Anglo-Saxon poetry, such as "The Ruin."

This is a deceptively simple poem. Its plain vocabulary was carefully chosen by the man who set the gold standard for dictionaries for the next two hundred years and who had by now set aside the pompous, erudite style of his prose writing.

Themes

Johnson had learned through years of freelance journalism and other writing that anyone submitting himself to his daily work was not only expecting to receive the results of his labor but was also running the risk of hoping too much. Social programs to help the unlucky were not reliable.

In the Bible, a parable tells of servants being given one talent (a measure of money) or ten talents by their master. Like one servant, Levet put his skills to good use and earned a worthy profit. In that parable, the master returns and scolds the servant who hid away the money instead of putting it to good use. Johnson is making a subtle warning here to the wealthy and talented to put their money and skills into worthy causes.

Commentary

This poem was written not only as a tribute to Johnson's friend but also as a literary response to *Lycidas* by Milton. Johnson felt that though that memorial lyric was respected as high art and grand writing, it was self-flattering to a sinful extent and unrealistic. Written in his later years, this is Johnson's considered response to *Lycidas*. It appeared when Johnson no longer had to write for a living—no one but a blockhead, he once said to his friend Boswell, writes but for money. He had the liberty not to care what anyone else thought of this poem.

Excerpt from *London*

. . . Here malice, rapine, accident conspire,
And now a rabble rages, now a fire;
Their ambush here relentless ruffians lay,
And here the fell attorney prowls for prey;
Here falling houses thunder on your head,
And here a female atheist talks you dead.
Here let those reign, whom pensions can incite
To vote a patriot black, a courtier white;
Explain their country's dear-bought rights away,
And plead for pirates in the face of day; . . .
Of all the griefs that harrass the distress'd,
Sure the most bitter is a scornfill jest;
Fate never wounds more deep the gen'rous heart
Than when a blockhead's insult points the dart....

This mournful truth is ev'ry where confess'd,
SLOW RISES WORTH, BY POVERTY DEPRESS'D ....

rapine—theft

fell—evil

Excerpt from
The Vanity of Human Wishes

Deign on the passing world to turn thine eyes,
And pause awhile from letters, to be wise;
There mark what ills the scholar's life assail,
Toil, envy, want, the patron, and the gaol.

...

The festal blazes, the triumphal show,
The ravish'd standard, and the captive foe,
The senate's thanks, the gazette's pompous tale,
With force resistless o'er the brave prevail.
Such bribes the rapid Greek o'er Asia whirl'd,
For such the steady Romans shook the world;
For such, in distant lands, the Britons shine,
And stain with blood the Danube or the Rhine;
This pow'r has praise, that virtue scarce can warm,
Till fame supplies the universal charm.
Yet reason frowns on war's unequal game,
Where wasted nations raise a single name;
And mortgag'd states, their grandsires wreaths regret.
From age to age in everlasting debt;
Wreaths which, at last, the dear-bought right convey
To rust on medals, or on stones decay.

deign—consider something worth your notice

gaol—jail

Critical Response To Johnson

With his first anonymously published poem, the satire *London*, Johnson was recognized even by Pope as a great talent. He became a phenomenal celebrity in his latter years. After meeting Johnson in 1763, the writer James Boswell was dazzled by the new prominence of this literary lion, quick-witted with barbed

James Boswell, the famed biographer of Johnson

punch lines though uncouth in dress. He wrote a biography that relied heavily upon anecdotes and conversations; many readers consider it a fine insight into the leading literary critic and scholar of his time, but Ford Maddox Ford called it "a fawning gesture of leechlike adoration of the greatest and most ridiculous of all biographers."[1] Many other biographies of Johnson appeared as well.

During the nineteenth century he was viewed as pompous and pedantic. The twentieth century saw Johnson's reputation taken seriously again. The latter half of the eighteenth century is referred to as "The Age of Johnson"—as the first half is considered the age of Pope and Swift.

Suggested Further Reading

Boswell's *The Life of Samuel Johnson LL.D.* (1791) is still read and held up as an example both of how to write and how not to write a useful and interesting biography.

One of Johnson's friends later in life was Fanny Burney, author of *Evelina*.

11

THOMAS GRAY

(1716–1771)

On December 26, 1716, at Cornhill, London, Thomas Gray was born in a small milliner's (hatmaker's) shop kept by his mother. He was the fifth of twelve children born to the unhappy marriage of Philip Gray, a money scrivener, and Dorothy Antrobus Gray, and the only one who survived infancy. In 1725, his mother sent young Thomas to her brothers in Cambridge.

There he was happy attending Eton College until 1734 and Peterhouse College until 1738, becoming close friends with Horace Walpole (son of the prime minister), Richard West, and Thomas Ashton. A small inheritance from his aunt gave Gray the financial freedom to leave college without finishing a degree. Gray began a Grand Tour of the Continent (a rite of passage for all young British men with the means to afford it) in 1739 with Walpole, but they quarreled in Italy. Returning to England in 1741, Gray resumed writing at his father's home. He sent his *Ode on Spring* and other poems to West in 1742 but was devastated to learn his dear friend had died unexpectedly.

He returned then to Peterhouse College, where he studied law. Most of his life was spent at Cambridge, studying Greek and writing academic works and poetry. He and Walpole reconciled in 1745, and Walpole's Strawberry Hill press later published Gray's *The Progress of Poetry* and *The Bard*. There were other close friendships, but he never married. Though he was made professor of history and modern languages in 1768 at Peterhouse College, he did no real teaching. Troubled by shyness and ill health, Gray lived very quietly, enjoying the company of his few friends rather than public crowds. He was a great letter writer in an age well known for correspondence.

He was planning to visit a close friend in Switzerland but fell ill and died July 30, 1771, at the age of fifty-five. Gray was buried at Stoke Poges beside his mother. There is a monument to his memory in Poets' Corner in Westminster Abbey, next to the monuments to Milton and Spenser.

FACTS

Taking Note

During his Grand Tour of France and Italy, Gray studied Latin and Italian writers, took notes in picture galleries, and visited churches. He began a careful habit of always recording his impressions on the spot, and afterward advised others to do so as well. Not all of his poems were grim or gloomy; Gray wrote about incidents in his life and among his acquaintances with humor and insight, as in the poem about Walpole's cat.

Excerpt from

Elegy Written in a Country Churchyard

The Curfew tolls the knell of parting day,
The lowing herd wind slowly o'er the lea,
The plowman homeward plods his weary way,
And leaves the world to darkness and to me.

Now fades the glimmering landscape on the sight,
And all the air a solemn stillness holds,
Save where the beetle wheels his droning flight,
And drowsy tinklings lull the distant folds;

Save that from yonder ivy-mantled tow'r
The moping owl does to the moon complain
Of such as, wand'ring near her secret bow'r,
Molest her ancient solitary reign.

Beneath those rugged elms, that yew-tree's shade,
Where heaves the turf in many a mould'ring heap,
Each in his narrow cell for ever laid,
The rude Forefathers of the hamlet sleep.

The breezy call of incense-breathing Morn,
The swallow twitt'ring from the straw-built shed,
The cock's shrill clarion, or the echoing horn,
No more shall rouse them from their lowly bed.

For them no more the blazing hearth shall burn,
Or busy housewife ply her evening care:
No children run to lisp their sire's return,
Or climb his knees the envied kiss to share.

Oft did the harvest to their sickle yield,
Their furrow oft the stubborn glebe has broke:
How jocund did they drive their team afield!
How bow'd the woods beneath their sturdy stroke!

Let not Ambition mock their useful toil,
Their homely joys, and destiny obscure;
Nor Grandeur hear with a disdainful smile
The short and simple annals of the poor.

The boast of heraldry, the pomp of pow'r,
And all that beauty, all that wealth e'er gave,
Awaits alike th' inevitable hour.
The paths of glory lead but to the grave.

glebe—meadow

Summary and Explication

Gray is describing a country village scene as evening approaches. The evening church bell rings to announce that the gate will soon be locked. Cows are returning from the meadow, and a farmer from the field, leaving the poet alone. It is getting dark and quiet, except for a buzzing beetle and metal tools clanking in the valley barnyards. There is an owl in the bell tower, near the cemetery.

The people in the graves will not wake up for morning church services, birdsong and roosters, or a hunting horn. No homes are waiting for them. They were good workers, and honored noblemen should not mock them. Even rich people die, too.

In the rest of the poem, Gray describes the grave of an unnamed young man and reads the epitaph.

Poetic Techniques

These short verses of four lines are written in iambic pentameter, giving a formal tone. The first and third lines rhyme, as do the second and fourth lines, in an *abab* pattern like a folk song. Gray structures his sentences in these verses in a style that was already old-fashioned, with artificial formalities and precision.

The line later in the poem "Far from the madding crowd's ignoble strife" evokes both Shakespeare's line "Fear no more the heat of the sun" and Chaucer's "Flee fro the prees and dwelle with soothfastnesse"—a tricky but successful turn of tone. Both poems would have been familiar to educated readers in Gray's day as in ours.

Themes

As the poem opens, light is fading from the world and the poet is left alone among graves. The theme of the end of life is told here solemnly but with a showy form of melancholy, like lyrics from modern songwriters Johnny Rotten or Kurt Cobain. And for a second theme in this excerpt, there is the warning worthy of the Bible's book of Ecclesiastes: Temporal power will not keep the rich from dying like the poor.

Commentary

Gray had been writing intense poetry, struggling with his readings of Milton's work and with a morbid sense of foreboding. With the untimely death of West, he knew anguish and resentment. He did not write a grand elegy glorifying a young hero in formal and classical terms, as Milton wrote *Lycidas*, though the final, revised version of the "Elegy" owes more to Milton than the original version does to the classic Roman poet Horace. Instead, Gray took almost ten years meditating on and revising his description of the grave of an unnamed young man, laid to rest in a humble place among worthy but unvalued people.

The dead man goes unnamed here and in the following poem (now listed in Gray's works as "On the Death of Richard West") as part of Gray's lifelong practice of keeping his love for West very private. Biographers of Gray acknowledge that he was homosexual but that he kept that fact from all but a very few dear friends.

One of the most quoted poems in English, "Elegy Written in a Country Churchyard" was published in haste, anonymously, to thwart a pirate edition. "It remains the most celebrated poem of its century," wrote Alexander Huber, and it "enjoyed an unusually wide and comprehensive audience."[1] It went through more than eleven printings and was thoroughly imitated, satirized, translated, and pirated. Gray never accepted payment from the publisher. The poem is still read and analyzed in at least two different editions.

Critical Response To Gray

All of Gray's poetry published before his death amounted to less than a thousand lines, but he was admired and influential out of all proportion to this modest body of work and far beyond his ambitions. In 1757, Gray was offered the post of poet laureate but refused it because the position was no longer an honor and the previous holder was a laughingstock.

On the Death of Richard West

In vain to me the smiling Mornings shine,
And reddening Phœbus lifts his golden fire;
The birds in vain their amorous descant join;
Or cheerful fields resume their green attire;
These ears, alas! for other notes repine,
A different object do these eyes require;
My lonely anguish melts no heart but mine;
And in my breast the imperfect joys expire.
Yet Morning smiles the busy race to cheer,
And new-born pleasure brings to happier men;
The fields to all their wonted tribute bear;
To warm their little loves the birds complain;
I fruitless mourn to him that cannot hear,
And weep the more because I weep in vain.

During roughly 1745 to 1785, "the age of sensibility" marked a transitional period in English literature, away from the detached satire of Pope and toward introspection and personal thoughts and feelings as a subject matter for poetry. Like other mid-century writers, Gray was fascinated with death and Gothic thoughts of the morbid, macabre, and melancholic. Samuel Johnson was relieved to be able to discuss Gray's "Elegy" with praise (in a biography that condemned Gray's artifice),[2] because he was well aware how many readers praised the poem's *sensibility*—the awareness of and willingness to discuss senses and feelings but to control them with classical ideas of restraint and composure. Gray was a strong influence upon the romantic poets, and his interest in natural landscapes and rural life anticipates Wordsworth's fascination with nature.

Ode on the Death of a Favourite Cat Drowned in a Tub of Goldfishes

'Twas on a lofty vase's side,
Where China's gayest art had dyed
The azure flowers that blow;
Demurest of the tabby kind
The pensive Selima, reclin'd,
Gazed on the lake below.

Her conscious tail her joy declared;
The fair round face, the snowy beard,
The velvet of her paws,
Her coat that with the tortoise vies,
Her ears of jet, and emerald eyes—
She saw, and purr'd applause.

Still had she gazed; but 'midst the tide
Two angel forms were seen to glide,
The Genii of the stream;
Their scaly armour's Tyrian hue
Through richest purple, to the view
Betray'd a golden gleam.

The hapless Nymph with wonder saw:
A whisker first, and then a claw
With many an ardent wish
She stretch'd, in vain, to reach the prize—
What female heart can gold despise?
What Cat's averse to fish?

Presumptuous maid! with looks intent
Again she stretch'd, again she bent,
Nor knew the gulf between—
Malignant Fate sat by, and smiled—
The slippery verge her feet beguiled,
She tumbled headlong in!

Eight times emerging from the flood
She mew'd to ev'ry watery God,
Some speedy aid to send:—
No Dolphin came, no Nereid stirr'd.
Nor cruel Tom nor Susan heard—
A favourite has no friend!

From hence, ye Beauties! undeceiv'd
Know one false step is ne'er retrieved,
And be with caution bold.
Not all that tempts your wandering eyes
And heedless hearts, is lawful prize,
Nor all that glisters, gold!

Nereid—a sea nymph

glisters—glistens

Thomas Gray

Suggested Further Reading

Reading Gray's collected works does not take long. Another of the poets of this time was William Collins. Jane Austen's novels focus on the age of sensibility, though she was writing a generation later. A modern biography and analysis worth reading is Robert F. Gleckner's *Gray Agonistes: Thomas Gray and Masculine Friendship,* which examines the influence of Milton's career and achievement on Gray as well as Gray's friendships and homosexual orientation.

WILLIAM BLAKE

(1757–1827)

Born into the family of a hosier (a tradesman who sells knitwear and hose) on November 28, 1757, in London, William Blake was given no formal education. He was apprenticed to James Basire, an engraver.

Blake was self-taught and a very impatient reader, except of the King James Bible and of Milton's poetry. "Blake was primarily an intellectual revisionist … of the European Enlightenment," says Harold Bloom, as were Nietzsche, Marx, and Freud, seeking "to correct the Enlightenment and not to abolish it. He had no quarrel with reason itself but only with inadequate accounts of reason."[1]

Blake's goals as he studied, wrote, and made engravings were to rescue English culture from what he interpreted as its decadence. He wanted to restore poetry to what it had been in the time of Milton and the Renaissance writers and raise English art to the standard of the spiritual art of Michelangelo and Raphael. In Blake's view, the Miltonizing poets of Sensibility failed "because they were not sane enough to overthrow a worldview Blake regarded as totally mad, and which he associated with Bacon, Newton, and Locke in metaphysics and with Dryden, Pope, Dr. Samuel Johnson, and Sir Joshua Reynolds in the arts."[2] His own works were the first of what we would now consider a modern style, hard for his contemporaries to understand, but were later to inspire the romantic poets.

Blake married Catherine Boucher in 1782. He and his wife were virtual recluses, living precariously on the few commissions he took as an engraver. Though their marriage was childless and suffered intense difficulties and poverty, it endured lifelong, and they eventually became close partners. Catherine was at his side on the Sunday evening of August 12, 1827, when Blake died, a very happy man.

FACTS

Blake and Social Justice

Born a member of the lower classes, Blake remained sensitive to their sufferings and defiantly loyal to them as a radical Protestant. In his notebooks and poems he raged against injustices and what he saw as the sins of the English conservative cultural traditions. Speaking his mind in public defied his patrons and caused him and his wife to suffer from poverty. "Blake learned the joyless wisdom of public timidity," says Harold Bloom.[3] When Blake angrily threw a rude soldier out of his garden, he found himself tried for treason, an expensive and emotional ordeal even though he was acquitted. The terror of this event had a profound effect upon his greatest poem, *Jerusalem*.

The Chimney-Sweeper

When my mother died I was very young,
And my father sold me while yet my tongue
Could scarcely cry "Weep! weep! weep! weep!"
So your chimneys I sweep, and in soot I sleep.

There's little Tom Dacre, who cried when his head,
That curled like a lamb's back, was shaved; so I said,
"Hush, Tom! Never mind it, for when your head's bare,
You know that the soot cannot spoil your white hair."

And so he was quiet, and that very night
As Tom was a-sleeping, he had such a sight!—
That thousands of sweepers, Dick, Joe, Ned and Jack,
Were all of them locked up in coffins of black.

And by came an angel, who had a bright key,
And he opened the coffins and set them all free;
Then down a green plain, leaping, laughing, they run
And wash in a river, and shine in the sun.

Then naked and white, all their bags left behind,
They rise upon clouds, and sport in the wind;
And the angel told Tom, if he'd be a good boy,
He'd have God for his father, and never want joy.

And so Tom awoke, and we rose in the dark,
And got with our bags and our brushes to work.
Though the morning was cold, Tom was happy and warm;
So if all do their duty, they need not fear harm.

Summary and Explication

Blake is writing here from the viewpoint of an unnamed small boy. When his mother died, his father sold him to be a chimney sweeper. The boy sweepers' heads were shaved to minimize lice and fleas and the chance of catching fire from sparks. One boy, Tom, dreamed of many sweepers locked in coffins till an angel set them free. They played on a green field, washed clean in a river, and played in the sky with no work or burdens. The angel told Tom that if he was good, God would be his father and he would never be unhappy. Tom woke and the sweepers went to work in the cold of an early morning, but Tom was comforted by his dream. If all of us do our duty we do not need to fear being punished.

Poetic Techniques

This poem is written in pairs of rhyming couplets, in a formal style for such a humble subject. Each verse has four lines of anapestic tetrameter, four feet with two unstressed syllables followed by a stressed syllable. There is some variation in the number of unstressed syllables. The third line in particular, where the child is lisping "weep! weep! weep! weep!" can be scanned as either iambic beats or four slow spondees.

In Blake's day, young children worked as chimney sweeps and in other dangerous jobs.

William Blake

Themes

In Blake's time, it was not uncommon for orphans or motherless children to be put to work for a living. The boy could have felt he was being sold as a slave, when he was calling out "sweep!" at a yearly job fair in a small town or square, where most laborers went to find employment, and fathers routinely pocketed the shilling of incentive pay. Boy chimney sweepers received no wages other than minimal food and a place to lie down. Chimneys would need to be swept at least once a year, so sweepers went round from building to building in towns and cities. They did not tend to live long.

The dream angel is not avenging, but lets the boys free to run and play, promising these orphans God for a father and happiness. Clean of the soot and ashes, they are naked and white. Black in this poem refers to the greasy, tarry soot covering all the boys like funeral garments. White refers to cleanliness and naturalness, like Tom's curly fair hair.

Commentary

Some modern readers, when first introduced to this poem, see Blake's black and white theme as racist, but the author had no hateful intent. One of the things that made Blake the first of the modern poets was that he was willing to write about people of other races, or children, or workers, as if their experiences mattered. The idea that anyone other than educated, upper-class adults had minds and feelings worth considering caused controversy. This poem was also controversial because Blake was writing here about the horror of children going without basic parental care after miserably hard work. A year earlier, in 1788, Parliament had passed a law insisting that "climbing boys" must be at least eight years old when apprenticed, they must be washed once a week, and they could not be forced to go up an ignited chimney.

Blake was not pleased by the morals of a religion that advised children and workers to do their service in hopes of heavenly comforts but allowed religious homeowners and businessmen to use up the health and lives of children and workers in service. He ends the poem with a brief but firm warning that those who do their duty do not need to fear being punished, implying that the reader has a duty to care for these exploited children. Some literary critics, religious leaders, and readers praised Blake's morality in this poem; others shunned it and said the matter was not fit for poetry or polite discussion. The Industrial Revolution was at hand, but the belief that children could be used up in hard work and abandoned without mercy was already old.

The Garden of Love

I went to the Garden of Love,
And saw what I never had seen:
A Chapel was built in the midst,
Where I used to play on the green.

And the gates of this Chapel were shut,
And 'Thou shalt not' writ over the door;
So I turned to the Garden of Love,
That so many sweet flowers bore.

And I saw it was filled with graves,
And tombstones where flowers should be;
And priests in black gowns were walking their rounds,
And binding with briars my joys and desires.

Commentary

Blake was a reverent believer in God and Christ, very appreciative of the beauty of the natural world. In his opinion, a religion that constructed chapels to control and administer religious observances should not do so at the expense of the natural world and shared green spaces. The chapel in this poem is closed, not open for services, and it bears a warning against being active and making choices. The garden where the narrator used to play is no longer filled with flowers but graves instead, and it is patrolled by priests like prison guards. The choice of the word *briars* instead of thorns is not only for the rhyme with *desires*; in England, where the land has been cultivated for thousands of years, the only places briars grow are wastelands, neglected and not put to good use.

Blake was an artist as well as a poet. This shows his engraving for the title page of a book by Edward Yung.

Critical Response To Blake

Blake was a controversial writer in his day, because several of his poems insisted that people of other races had minds and feelings as did English people, contrary to common racist beliefs at the time. He also believed that children and working people had thoughts and feelings every bit as worth consideration as those of powerful lords. Though some of the phrasing in his poetry may appear by modern standards to be rather patronizing, Blake idealized a future and a heaven with racial equality and brotherhood.

The Tyger

Tyger! Tyger! burning bright
In the forests of the night;
What immortal hand or eye
Could frame thy fearful symmetry?

In what distant deeps or skies
Burnt the fire of thine eyes?
On what wings dare he aspire?
What the hand, dare seize the fire?

And what shoulder, & what art,
Could twist the sinews of thy heart,
And when thy heart began to beat,
What dread hand? & what dread feet?

What the hammer? What the chain?
In what furnace was thy brain?
What the anvil? What dread grasp
Dare its deadly terrors clasp?

When the stars threw down their spears
And water'd heaven with their tears,
Did he smile his work to see?
Did he who made the Lamb make thee?

Tyger! Tyger! burning bright,
In the forests of the night,
What immortal hand or eye
Dare frame thy fearful symmetry?

"Blake was regarded as a scrappy eccentric who had proved to be consistently difficult in all business dealings," according to James King's biography.[4] Most of his poetry was illustrated with his own drawings, paintings, and engravings in a style that was not then commercially successful, though from a modernist or postmodernist viewpoint, it has merit. This makes Blake almost unique, for writers who illustrate their own work tend not to succeed as published authors or artists. He received modest recognition of his talents later in life and had a profound influence upon the romantic poets and again in the twentieth century.

Suggested Further Reading

Two collections of Blake's poetry still studied today are *Songs of Innocence* and *Songs of Experience.* A biography that puts Blake into context with his time and with other writers is *William Blake: His Life,* by James King. Among Blake's contemporaries were novelist Fanny Burke and essayist Mary Wollstonecraft.

13

WILLIAM WORDSWORTH
(1770–1850)

On April 7, 1770, William Wordsworth was born in Cockermouth, Cumberland, in the Lake District in northwest England. His father was John Wordsworth, attorney to Sir James Lowther. The children in the family were separated and sent to live with several different relatives when their mother died in 1778, and they were orphaned when their father died five years later. These losses separated young William not only from his family but also from the Lake District, whose mountains and wild countryside had already affected his imagination deeply and given him a love of nature.

Young William entered a local school with the help of two uncles. In 1787, a sonnet of his was published in *The European Magazine*, and he went on to St. John's College in Cambridge University. Much interested in the French Revolution, Wordsworth went on a summer walking tour in France and Switzerland in 1790 before finishing his degree in 1791. On a second trip to France, Wordsworth had an affair with Annette Vallon, daughter of a French barber-surgeon. Though they had an illegitimate daughter, Wordsworth returned to England, financially unable to

William Wordsworth

support a family. He wrote a poem, "Vaudracour and Julia," based on this affair but otherwise did his best to hide the matter.

In 1795 he met Samuel Taylor Coleridge, and they recognized each other as kindred spirits, inspired by the French and American revolutions and full of radical ideas about morality, such as allowing young women and men to associate and travel together without being married. They resolved to create poetry that spoke from the heart and imagination. That year, Wordsworth inherited a small legacy on the death of a friend. With this modest income, he settled in a small house with his sister Dorothy at Racedown, Dorset. Living in the Lake District stimulated his imagination by close contact with nature. Frequent meetings with Coleridge led to the creation and publication of their great work together, *Lyrical Ballads*. This collection of poems by Wordsworth and poems by Coleridge was the subject of much literary discussion and controversy. Wordsworth began composing a philosophical and autobiographical poem in 1798 and completed it more or less in 1805, though he was never perfectly satisfied. *The Prelude* was published posthumously.

Wordsworth spent the winter of 1798–1799 traveling in Germany with his sister and Coleridge. There he wrote several poems, among them the "Lucy" poems, subtle and mysterious. After their return, Wordsworth and his sister Dorothy moved to Dove Cottage, Grasmere, in the center of the Lake District. When Wordsworth married Mary Hutchison in 1802, their marriage was an emotional upheaval for Dorothy. Even so, she continued to live with them for the rest of her life. In 1835 her health deteriorated; William and his family nursed her for the next twenty years.

In 1807, Wordsworth's second verse collection, *Poems, In Two Volumes*, was published. When he was appointed to a civil service position as official distributor of stamps for Westmoreland (a county in the Lake District), Wordsworth moved the family from Grasmere in 1813 to Rydal Mount, Ambleside. He lived there for the rest of his life, having abandoned the radical, revolutionary ideas of his youth to become a conservative patriot in public life. In 1843 he became England's poet laureate. He died on April 23, 1850.

I Wander'd Lonely as a Cloud

I wander'd lonely as a cloud
That floats on high o'er vales and hills,
When all at once I saw a crowd,
A host, of golden daffodils;
Beside the lake, beneath the trees,
Fluttering and dancing in the breeze.

Continuous as the stars that shine
And twinkle on the Milky Way,
They stretch'd in never-ending line
Along the margin of a bay:
Ten thousand saw I at a glance
Tossing their heads in sprightly dance.

The waves beside them danced, but they
Out-did the sparkling waves in glee:
A poet could not but be gay,
In such a jocund company:
I gazed—and gazed—but little thought
What wealth the show to me had brought.

For oft, when on my couch I lie
In vacant or in pensive mood,
They flash upon that inward eye
Which is the bliss of solitude;
And then my heart with pleasure fills,
And dances with the daffodils.

jocund—cheerful

Summary and Explication

The poet is describing taking a lonely walk in the hills and valleys and seeing a field of daffodils by a lake. The flowers moved in the breeze. There were as many as stars in the sky. It was a cheerful sight. And later, when lying indoors bored or thoughtful, the poet remembers that joy.

Poetic Techniques

These four verses of six lines each seem deceptively simple. The last syllables of the lines rhyme in the pattern *ababcc*. Each line of iambic quatrameter has four stressed syllables, like many ballads and almost like the pattern of the poetry of the Anglo-Saxons. It is a pattern of oral poetry rather than the literary poetry written in iambic pentameter blank verse of Shakespeare and Milton.

The words are mostly plain and simple. The statements of the poem are almost direct enough for a poem by George Herbert. But poetry of this style is not a flat statement of what is seen, as Herbert wrote. The romantics largely wrote what is called lyrical verse, as the poet describes a moment's feelings in detail and acutely, so as to help the reader have a similar image in his or her own "inward eye."

Themes

Merely being afoot in the natural world is enough to inspire the poet. Wordsworth was not so much an intellectual or a Christian as a naturalist, saying of himself in his strongest poem, "Lines Composed a Few Miles Above Tintern Abbey":

> . . . well pleased to recognise
> In nature and the language of the sense,
> The anchor of my purest thoughts, the nurse,
> The guide, the guardian of my heart, and soul
> Of all my moral being.

The final verse of the daffodil poem mentions being refreshed by the memory of these daffodils when lying indoors, bored or thoughtful. Both Wordsworth and

Dorothy suffered from what was then called melancholy and would now be recognized as clinical depression. It is debatable whether they would have thrived in a modern world with twenty-first-century morals, even with psychotherapy and medications to relieve depression. But clearly both had learned the virtue of making and recalling memories of joyful moments to brighten idle or thoughtful moods and to bring some relief of melancholy.

FACTS

William and Dorothy

Literary critics who knew both William Wordsworth and his sister Dorothy regarded her as having a finer mind and talent for poetry. But she spent all her talents assisting her brother for ten years during the creation of his most celebrated poetry. Dorothy was not only Wordsworth's homemaker before his marriage, she was also his assistant, preparing readable copies of all his work and taking dictation when he developed psychosomatic pains on picking up a pen. He frequently asked her to read from the journals she kept of their home life, rambles, and travels together, and he used her notes when composing. Several of his poems are based upon her experiences, not his own or shared events. Dorothy was encouraged by literary friends to prepare her journals for publication but never did. Their literary partnership ended in the early years of Wordsworth's marriage, and the writing of his middle and later years was less well regarded by critics. Wordsworth's most celebrated poetry would be better considered the product of their collaboration, rather than his work alone or hers under his name.

The Wordsworths' home in England's Lake District

Commentary

This poem in particular is a paraphrase of an entry in Dorothy's journal. "Many of William's poems originated in incidents recorded in Dorothy's journal," wrote Kathleen Jones in her book on the sisters, wives, and daughters of the Lake Poets:

> … In conversation with the poet Aubrey Vere, he criticized the poet who "went out with his pencil and notebook, and jotted down whatever struck him most." The poet should have "observed, thought, felt" and then when he got home, "after several days had passed by, he should have interrogated his memory." That his own memory had been constantly refreshed by Dorothy's jottings had been conveniently forgotten, and his earlier admissions that it was through Dorothy's eyes he saw nature were now denied.[1]

Written at a small distance from my House, and sent by my little boy to the person to whom they are addressed.

It is the first mild day of March:
Each minute sweeter than before
The red-breast sings from the tall larch
That stands beside our door.

There is a blessing in the air,
Which seems a sense of joy to yield
To the bare trees, and mountains bare,
And grass in the green field.

My sister! ('tis a wish of mine)
Now that our morning meal is done,
Make haste, your morning task resign;
Come forth and feel the sun.

Edward will come with you; —and, pray,
Put on with speed your woodland dress;
And bring no book; for this one day
We'll give to idleness.

No joyless forms shall regulate
Our living calendar:
We from to-day, my Friend, will date
The opening of the year.

Love, now a universal birth,
From heart to heart is stealing,
From earth to man, from man to earth;
— It is the hour of feeling.

One moment now may give us more
Than fifty years of reason:
Our minds shall drink at every pore
The spirit of the season.

Some silent laws our hearts may make,
Which they shall long obey:
We for the year to come may take
Our temper from to-day.

And from the blessed power that rolls
About, below, above,
We'll frame the measure of our souls;
They shall be tuned to love.

Then come, my Sister! come, I pray,
With speed put on your woodland dress;
And bring no book: for this one day
We'll give to idleness.

Upon Westminster Bridge

Earth has not anything to show more fair:
    Dull would he be of soul who could pass by
    A sight so touching in its majesty:
This city now doth like a garment wear
The beauty of the morning; silent, bare,
Ships, towers, domes, theatres, and temples lie
Open unto the fields, and to the sky;
All bright and glittering in the smokeless air.
Never did sun more beautifully steep
    In his first splendour valley, rock, or hill;
Ne'er saw I, never felt, a calm so deep!
    The river glideth at his own sweet will:
Dear God! The very houses seem asleep;
    And all that mighty heart is lying still!

Critical Response To Wordsworth

Wordsworth became the defining member of the English romantic movement among poets, along with his colleague Coleridge, with the publication of their joint work, *Lyrical Ballads*. Deeply influenced by his love of nature, like the other romantics, Wordsworth's personality and poetry were shaped by the sights and scenes of the Lake Country. ("Romance" is derived from the French word *roman*, for a tale of exciting adventures and mysterious events, not merely the simple love stories sold as twentieth- or twenty-first-century romance novels.) He became an example for others who wrote about their own experiences and beloved places. The poetry of Wordsworth and the romantics was held in high regard during their lives and has been discussed and admired ever since.

SuggesTed FurTher Reading

As one of the romantic poets, Wordsworth should not overshadow his colleague Coleridge, or Robert Southey and other poets of the Lake Country. The changing standards of social morals of their time are discussed in many contemporary books, such as the essays of Mary Wollstonecraft. An excellent biography by Kathleen Jones, *A Passionate Sisterhood: The Sisters, Wives and Daughters of the Lake Poets,* gathers telling details not only of the lives of Wordsworth, Coleridge, and their associates but also of the women in their families whose lives were deeply affected by these men and their intellectual, poetic, and moral beliefs.

14

JOHN KEATS

(1795–1821)

John Keats was born on October 31, 1795, the first son of Thomas Keats and Frances Jennings Keats. Frances Jennings's parents owned a prosperous livery called "The Swan and Hoop," where horses and transportation were for hire, and Thomas Keats ran the stable.

Young John went away to school in 1803. A year later, a fall from a horse killed his father. Within two months, his mother made a disastrous marriage to William Rawlings, a London bank clerk. Frances soon fled Rawlings, who sold The Swan and Hoop and disappeared. Frances's mother, Alice Jennings, took custody of her grandchildren. During this upsetting time, John began getting into fistfights. Though small, he rarely lost a fight.

In 1809, his mother, Frances, returned to the family, suffering from illness and depression. John was delighted, but his devoted care could not cure tuberculosis, or consumption as it was called then. Frances Keats died in 1810. Young John took her death very hard. A year later, he was apprenticed to Thomas Hammond, a surgeon living in the neighborhood.

Keats began reading lyric poetry in 1813, including Sir Edmund Spenser's *The Faerie Queene.* He also began rebelling against Hammond, disagreeing with him on politics and other matters. Something of a libertarian at this time, Keats had democratic and antiauthoritarian ideals. Keats lived alone, writing poetry while continuing his medical studies. He later burned almost all his early work.

A sketch of John Keats by R. R. Haydn, done in 1816

In 1816, his first published sonnets appeared in *The Examiner,* a liberal newspaper. This established him with the critics and in the public eye as a fine poet. Keats's first book was published on March 3, 1817, but sales were not encouraging. Percy Bysshe Shelley challenged him to a contest writing epic poetry, and that summer Keats wrote *Endymion.* That year, Keats was the most sought-after young poet at parties and dances in London, though he did not like crowds.

Keats set himself a ten-year plan to learn the talents of the great poets, such as Shakespeare and Milton, without becoming derivative. In five years of published

Year of Wonder

Keats enjoyed a strenuous walking tour in the spring and summer of 1818, through the English Lake Country, Scotland, and Ireland. The prolonged wet, cold weather gave him chills, and he developed a chronic sore throat. That fall, Keats nursed his younger brother, Tom, dying of tuberculosis. His other brother, George, had just married and emigrated to Kentucky, but because of bad investments needed whatever money Keats could earn and send him. During this time, Keats also fell in love with Fanny Brawne but was never able to marry her.

In spite of these stresses, Keats was still able to achieve the finest of his poetry. From January to September 1819, he wrote an astonishing series of mature poems: lyric verses, six great odes, and fine sonnets. It was a year of emotional turmoil and a year of phenomenal creativity matched by no other English poet, before or since. Later critics refer to this as his year of wonder, or *annus mirabilis.*

work he drove himself hard, though he was hampered by depression and poverty. He realized in early 1820 that he was likely to die soon from tuberculosis like his mother and brother. Weakened by hemorrhages, in his last months he was unable to continue working. Friends brought him to Italy for the milder climate, but he died in Rome on February 23, 1821. All that he wanted written on his gravestone was "Here lies one whose name was writ in water."

On First Looking into Chapman's Homer

Much have I travell'd in the realms of gold,
And many goodly states and kingdoms seen;
Round many western islands have I been
Which bards in fealty to Apollo hold.
Oft of one wide expanse had I been told
That deep-brow'd Homer ruled as his demesne:
Yet did I never breathe its pure serene
Till I heard Chapman speak out loud and bold:
Then felt I like some watcher of the skies
When a new planet swims into his ken;
Or like stout Cortez, when with eagle eyes
He star'd at the Pacific—and with all his men
Look'd at each other with a wild surmise—
Silent, upon a peak in Darien.

fealty—loyalty to a feudal lord
demesne (pronounced "di-MEAN")—domain

Summary and Explication

Keats is writing here of his feelings studying classical poetry. He has traveled in his mind to many interesting places from these valued books, including some islands of Greece where the sun god Apollo was worshiped by poet-priests. He has heard about the grand stories that Homer told best of all. But he never felt that he was breathing the air of that place and time till he read George Chapman's translation into English of Homer's epic poems the *Iliad* and the *Odyssey*. Then he felt like an astronomer discovering a new planet. He felt like a strong explorer climbing a mountain in Panama with his team, the first Europeans to see the Pacific Ocean and guess what it could hold.

Poetic Techniques

In this sonnet, the last syllable of each line rhymes with other lines in the pattern *abba abba cdcdcd*. (The first line, *a*, rhymes with the fourth line, the fifth, and the eighth.)

Keats is writing about intellectual discovery. He opens the poem with a metaphor: He talks about travel to foreign countries to describe how he has learned much from studying the poetry of those places. He closes the poem with a simile based on that metaphor of travel, saying that he feels like the first European explorer to see a vast new ocean.

Themes

The first theme in this sonnet is the awe that Keats and other British scholars felt for Greek and Roman classical writings. Travel was not something Keats could afford, because his small inheritance was being withheld until he turned twenty-five. The "realms of gold" he visited were books written in foreign countries. Did he call the books "realms of gold" because the edges of the paper were gilded? Or because he valued their contents?

The second theme is the awe that Keats has for discovery of the physical world through modern sciences and exploration. The feeling he gets from reading

Chapman's translation is as astonishing and wonderful as finding a new planet with a telescope, as when William and Catherine Herschel had discovered Uranus in 1781. (In a later poem, *Lamia*, Keats referred to Newton's studies of optical lenses.) Even more, his awe feels like climbing a mountain with brave companions to discover a vast new world ready to explore.

Commentary

When Keats's former schoolteacher Charles Cowden Clarke showed him a robust translation of Homer by the Elizabethan poet George Chapman, they read it together all night long. Keats walked home at dawn. He wrote this sonnet, and it was delivered to Clarke by the ten o'clock post that morning.

This sonnet is Keats's first great poem. Within weeks of this poem's publication in *The Examiner*, editor and critic Leigh Hunt wrote an article praising the poetry of both Keats and Percy Bysshe Shelley. This sonnet was praised then because it shows what was considered a proper respect for knowledge from ancient Greece. Also, scientific studies were bringing whole new kinds of discoveries to public awareness. And wealthy people still hoped to find many opportunities for financial gain as exploration and colonization of the New World was proceeding. The themes of this poem were very much to the taste of educated readers in 1816. One fact is wrong—the explorer who climbed Darien in Panama was Balboa, not Cortez.

A marble bust of the Greek poet Homer. A translation of his work inspired one of Keats's most famous poems.

Where's the Poet?

Where's the Poet? show him! show him,
Muses nine! that I may know him.
'Tis the man who with a man
Is an equal, be he King,
Or poorest of the beggar-clan
Or any other wonderous thing
A man may be 'twixt ape and Plato;
'Tis the man who with a bird,
Wren or Eagle, finds his way to
All its instincts; he hath heard
The Lion's roaring, and can tell
What his horny throat expresseth,
And to him the Tiger's yell
Comes articulate and presseth
On his ear like mother-tongue.

Summary and Explication

Keats asks the nine Muses to show him what a poet is. To him, a poet is an equal with every man from king to beggar. A poet understands every animal instinct and intent of our nature. With his image of "any other wonderous thing / A man may be 'twixt ape and Plato," Keat upholds not only the ideas of Darwin's theory but also his own reverence for ancient Greek philosophy. He mentions animals, not scorned ones but Eagle and Lion, symbolic animals representing gods and kings, and calls to mind the great poets Pope and Blake by referring to Wren and Tiger.

This Living Hand, Now Warm and Capable

This living hand, now warm and capable
Of earnest grasping, would, if it were cold
And in the icy silence of the tomb,
So haunt thy days and chill thy dreaming nights
That thou wouldst wish thine own heart dry of blood,
So in my veins red life might stream again,
And thou be conscience-calm'd. See, here it is—
I hold it towards you.

Summary and Explication

Keats is writing of his own hand, now warm and alive, to some person who could hold that hand. If it were cold and he were dead, the person would think about it day and night. The person would be willing to die to bring back the poet's life, just to stop grieving. He is holding out his hand.

Poetic Techniques

Like many free verse poems, this poem is not constrained by rhymes at the end of lines or alliteration. There is some attention paid to the selection of vowel sounds, as two or more short vowels are usually followed by a longer vowel. The effect slows down the pace of reading, so the lines are not rushed. The consonance of "icy silence" and "conscience-calm'd" stands out. These lines are not forced into end rhyme and obvious patterns.

This short verse has the most thoroughly modern appearance of all Keats's poems. Yet it also brings to mind the anonymous Old English poems "Deor" and "Wulf and Eadwacer." A thousand years before this poem was written, those old poems were similarly grim in tone and also used a short line for emphasis. But here, instead of four stresses per line, these lines are composed in iambic pentameter.

Themes

The theme of death as something to be feared dominates these few lines. Death could be right at hand. It is frightening for those left behind. One would rather be dead than be alive if the poet were dead.

The poem is a glimpse inside the mind of a man trained as a medical doctor and a surgeon. Doctors are often troubled by thoughts of people they could not help. Medical transfusions were not reliable then. But the theme of a person allowing his or her blood to be drained into a dead person to restore life is older than modern medicine: the vampire myth.

Critical Commentary

These lines were found written on a blank part of a page of a poem Keats left unfinished. Some biographers assume he was addressing these words to Fanny Brawne, his fiancée. Others suggest that this was a note for a drama he was planning. At any rate, this is not a poem about death as a great mystery that comes to all. It is an attempt to make the person addressed think and feel as the poet does about his own coming death.

In Keats's day, people often died in accidents or from illnesses that can now be cured. He nursed his mother and brother, and he diagnosed his own symptoms of tuberculosis. But this poem does not whine and complain. It ends with the poet holding out his hand to the person he is addressing. Surely, this is an offer to put this still warm and capable hand to use, in what Harold Bloom calls "the gift of tragic acceptance … of an outward world that would survive his perception of it."[1]

CriTicaL Response To KeaTs

Though Leigh Hunt praised Keats's early poetry in *The Examiner*, by 1818 *Blackwood Magazine* attacked him as a member of the "Cockney School," Hunt's radical literary circle. In addition, the *Quarterly Review* ran a savagely negative review of *Endymion*. Other poets, such as Byron and Shelley, believed the sentimental legend that Keats was a frail flower crushed by these articles. But Keats was critical of his own work in *Endymion* and resolved to improve.

In five years of published writing, Keats remained in the public eye. He died while his fully mature writing was still improving, with greater achievements by age twenty-four than anything done by Chaucer, Shakespeare, or Milton at the same age. Within fifty years of his death, his first biographies recognized what *The Norton Anthology of English Literature* calls "the immense waste of so extraordinary an intellect and genius cut off early."[2]

It was a radical act during his life to write from personal experience, like Blake and Wordsworth, but our contemporary poets rely upon it. Many modern rock stars and songwriters from Jim Morrison to Kurt Cobain and the band Evanescence have written songs heavily influenced by Keats's odes and longer poetry. The science fiction author Dan Simmons wrote his novel *Hyperion* and three sequels based on inspiration from Keats's *Hyperion* and *Endymion*.

Keats wrote about Lilith in his poem *Lamia*, developing the basis for the modern vampire story. This had an influence on Mary Shelley's novel *Frankenstein* and on the novel *Dracula* by Bram Stoker, which were the founding works of two modern genres of writing: science fiction and horror.

SuggesTed FurTher Reading

Other poets of that time included Percy Bysshe Shelley and George Gordon (Lord Byron). A contemporary novel that shows many of the same influences as Keats's poetry is *Frankenstein*, by Mary Shelley.

Chapter Notes

Chapter 1. Anglo-Saxon Poets (c. 600–1000)

1. Margaret Ferguson, Mary Jo Salter, and Jon Stallworthy, eds., *The Norton Anthology of Poetry*, 4th ed. (New York: W.W. Norton & Co., 1970), p. 1.

2. Michael Alexander, *The Earliest English Poems*, 2nd ed. (New York: Penguin Classics, 1977), p. 10.

3. Ibid., p. 7.

4. Ibid., p. 11.

5. Ibid., p. 7.

Chapter 2. Geoffrey Chaucer (c. 1342–1400)

1. Donald R. Howard, *Chaucer: His Life, His Works, His World* (New York: E.P. Dutton, NAL Penguin, 1987), p. 525.

2. Ibid.

Chapter 3. Anonymous Folk Songs (c. 1100–1600)

1. Cecil J. Sharp, *One Hundred English Folksongs* (New York: Dover Publications, 1916, 1944), p. xiii.

Chapter 4. Sir Edmund Spenser (1552–1599)

1. Harold Bloom, *The Best Poems of the English Language: From Chaucer Through Robert Frost* (New York: HarperCollins, 2004), pp. 59–60.

2. Andrew Zurcher, ed., "Biography," *The Edmund Spenser Homepage*, 2004, <http://www.english.cam.ac.uk/spenser/biography.htm> (July 20, 2007).

Chapter 5. William Shakespeare (1564–1616)

1. Smith and Lewalski, "William Shakespeare," in M. H. Abrams, et al., eds.,
    The Norton Anthology of English Literature, 5th ed., vol. 1 (Markham, Ontario:
    Penguin Books, Canada, 1962), p. 867.

2. Ibid.

Chapter 6. John Donne (1572–1631)

1. Brian Phillips, *SparkNotes on Donne's Poetry*, n.d., <http://www.
    sparknotes.com/poetry/donne> (August 1, 2007).

2. Harold Bloom, "John Donne," *The Best Poems of the English Language: From
    Chaucer Through Robert Frost* (New York: HarperCollins, 2004), p. 139.

Chapter 7. George Herbert (1593–1633)

1. Anniina Jokinen, "George Herbert (1593–1633)," *17th C. English Literature:
    Metaphysical Poets, Luminarium,* June 27, 2000,
    <http://www.luminarium.org/sevenlit/herbert/herbbio.htm> (November 11,
    2008).

2. Harold Bloom, "George Herbert," *The Best Poems of the English Language:
    From Chaucer Through Robert Frost* (New York: HarperCollins, 2004), p. 183.

3. George Herbert, "Jordan (II)," in Harold Bloom, *The Best Poems of the
    English: From Chaucer Throught Robert Frost Language* (New York:
    HarperCollins, 2004), p. 186.

Chapter 8. John Milton (1608–1674)

1. Anniina Jokinen, "John Milton (1608–1674)," *Religious Writers of the English
    Renaissance, Luminarium*, September 14, 2006, <http://www.
    luminarium.org/sevenlit/milton/> (June 20, 2007).

2. M. H. Sherman, "T. S. Eliot: His Religion, His Poetry, His Roles,"
    Psychoanalytical Review, 84:73–107, 1997.

Chapter 9. Alexander Pope (1688–1744)

1. David Cody, "Alexander Pope Biography," *Pre-Victorian Poets,* July 2000, <http://www.scholars.nus.edu.sg/landow/victorian/previctorian/pope/rape.html> (August 10, 2007).

2. Ibid.

Chapter 10. Samuel Johnson (1709–1784)

1. Petri Luikkonen, "Samuel Johnson (1709–1784)," *Books and Writers,* 2002, <http://www.kirjasto.sci.fi/samuelj.htm> (July 2, 2007).

Chapter 11. Thomas Gray (1716–1771)

1. Alexander Huber, ed., *Thomas Gray Archive*, August 7, 2007, <http://www.thomasgray.org/materials/bio.shtml> (August 18, 2007).

2. Harold Bloom, "Thomas Gray," *The Best Poems of the English Language: From Chaucer Through Robert Frost* (New York: HarperCollins, 2004), p. 282.

Chapter 12. William Blake (1757–1827)

1. Harold Bloom, "William Blake," *The Best Poems of the English Language: From Chaucer Through Robert Frost* (New York: HarperCollins, 2004), p. 302.

2. Ibid., p. 304.

3. Ibid.

4. James King, *William Blake: His Life* (London: George Weidenfeld and Nicolson Ltd, 1991), p. 210.

Chapter 13. William Wordsworth (1770–1850)

1. Kathleen Jones, *A Passionate Sisterhood: The Sisters, Wives and Daughters of the Lake Poets* (London: Virago Press, 1998), pp. 133–134.

Chapter 14. John Keats (1795–1821)

1. Harold Bloom, "John Keats," *The Best Poems of the English Language: From Chaucer Through Robert Frost* (New York: HarperCollins, 2004), p. 459.

2. M. H. Abrams et al., eds., *The Norton Anthology of English Literature*, 5th ed., vol. 1 (Markham, Ontario: Penguin Books, Canada, 1962), p. 987.

GLOSSARY

alliteration—The repetition of an initial consonant sound.

anapest—A metrical foot consisting of two unstressed syllables followed by one stressed syllable.

assonance—The selection of a word by its vowel sounds.

caesura (say-ZHU-ra)—A break in the flow of sound in a verse.

consonance—Harmony or agreement of sounds in words.

couplet—A pair of lines with end rhyme.

dactyl—A metrical foot consisting of one stressed syllable followed by two unstressed syllables.

dirge—A song of mourning at a funeral, to honor the dead and express grief.

doggerel—Casual verse, usually considered clumsy and with little artistic merit.

elegy—A poem expressing sorrow for one who has died, or a pensive, melancholy poem.

epithet—A word or phrase that accompanies a name or is used in its place.

female rhyme—Rhyme consisting of two or more syllables (such as pilaster/alabaster).

foot—The basic unit of verse meter in poetry; a unit of syllables within a line, with various numbers of stressed and unstressed syllables.

hexameter—A line of verse with six metrical feet.

iamb—A metrical foot consisting of one unstressed syllable followed by one stressed syllable.

imagery—Figurative language.

male rhyme—One-syllable rhyme (such as red/dead).

metaphor—A figure of speech in which a word is compared to another to suggest similarity between them.

metaphysical—A style of poetry that is highly philosophical and intellecutal and marked by unusual imagery.

meter—The measure of systematically arranged rhythm in poetry, in units of syllables within a line.

pastoral—In art and literature, a work dealing with shepherds, usually stressing the relative serenity and innocence of rural life compared to city life.

pentameter—A line of verse with five metrical feet.

rhyme—Choosing words by the final sound or sounds; lines of poetry may rhyme within the line or, more usually, at the end.

romanticism—A movement in art, music, and literature that emphasized emotion, nature, and the experience of common people.

satire—A literary work that holds up human weaknesses for ridicule.

scop (skope)—An Anglo-Saxon poet.

scrivener—A notary public; formerly functioned as law clerk, legal secretary, moneylender, or agent.

sensibility—Refined or excessive sensitivity in emotion or taste.

simile—A figure of speech in which two things are compared using the terms "like" or "as."

sonnet—A poem with fourteen lines of iambic pentameter verse, with a variety of rhyme patterns, based on an Italian form ("little song") made popular by Petrarch.

spondee—A metrical foot consisting of two stressed syllables.

stanza—A verse or set of lines grouped together and set apart from the rest of the poem, like a paragraph in prose writing.

symbol—Something that represents something else.

tetrameter—A line of verse with four metrical feet.

trochee—A metrical foot consisting of one stressed syllable followed by one unstressed syllable.

Further Reading

Books

Alexander, Michael. *The Earliest English Poems.* 2nd edition. New York: Penguin Classics, 1977.

Andronik, Catherine M. *Wildly Romantic: The English Romantic Poets— The Mad, the Bad, and the Dangerous.* New York: Henry Holt and Co., 2007.

Bloom, Harold. *The Best Poems of the English Language: Fom Chaucer Through Robert Frost.* New York: HarperCollins, 2004.

Morris, Jackie. *The Barefoot Book of Classic Poems.* Cambridge, Mass.: Barefoot Books, 2006.

Rossignol, Rosalyn. *Critical Companion to Chaucer: A Literary Reference to His Life and Work.* New York: Facts on File, 2006.

Streissguth, Tom. *Understanding Beowulf.* Detroit: Lucent Books, 2004.

Internet Addresses

Luminarium: Anthology of English Literature
<http://www.luminarium.org>

Poetry Foundation
<http://www.poetryfoundation.org>

Representative Poetry Online
<http://rpo.library.utoronto.ca/display/>